Heal Your Mind
and Your Body
Will Heal,
— Book 1 —

REV. DR. ALMA MARIE STEVENS

BALBOA.
PRESS

A DIVISION OF HAY HOUSE

Scripture taken from the King James Version of the Bible.

Balboa Press books may be ordered through booksellers or by contacting:

Balboa Press
A Division of Hay House
1663 Liberty Drive
Bloomington, IN 47403
www.balboapress.com
1 (877) 407-4847

Print information available on the last page.

ISBN: 978-1-5043-4529-3 (sc)
ISBN: 978-1-5043-4531-6 (hc)
ISBN: 978-1-5043-4530-9 (e)

Library of Congress Control Number: 2015919367

Balboa Press rev. date: 12/03/2015

Contents

PRAYERS

Acknowledgements

To Judy Jackson, Mya Fuller, Bennie Smith, (my brother) and Elaine Olson who helped in financing the production of this project. Doris Alvin, who took on the first proofing and supported this work, Tawnicia Ferguson Rowan, project manager and editor. Patricia Ann Murray and Melvin my daughter and son who have been the wind beneath my wings since I began this work. Anne Roberts and all the students who have used these prayers in their lives with positive results and inspired me to write this work for all people.

And God said, let us make man in our image, after our likeness, and let them have dominion over the fish of the sea, and over the fowl of the air, and over the cattle, and over all the earth, and over every creeping thing that creepeth upon the earth.

Genesis 1:25 KJV

Preface

Prayers are for the purpose of clearing the mind to receive an answer for an idea. The roots for directing our lives are our feelings, images, and thoughts.

Heal Your Mind and Your Body Will Heal is based upon Universal Laws that govern our feelings, images, and thoughts. We need to address our feelings, images, and thoughts to begin the process for complete restoration of our health. We have ignored our feelings, images, and thoughts because they are so complex that we simply cannot separate them.

Our Dedication is to the image in which we are all made—that part of us that can only be developed by recognizing the difference between our feelings, images, and thoughts. Most of us cannot identify our feelings. *Heal Your Mind and Your Body Will Heal* is designed to introduce the language that will help us develop the Image in which we are made. Because one of the ways we learn in by repetition, the repetition of these prayers brings about the restoration of our feelings, images, and thoughts to correctly identify them.

We recognize laws that govern our world. According to Dr. Raymond Fleet, author of *Bringers of the Dawn*, there are 12 Universal Laws that govern the Mind, and 12 Universal Laws that govern the Soul. There are 12 Universal Laws that govern beyond Mind, Soul, and Spirit. There are seven Universal Laws that govern the Spirit of every individual. These laws activate our feelings, images, and thoughts (FITs), which govern our lives. We cannot change our FITs until we know the cause of them. We do not scratch unless we itch.

Many of our physical, emotional, mental, and spiritual challenges stem from non-recognition of the purpose of these Laws. With repetition of the prayers in this book, you will see a change in how you view events, situations, conditions, and Dis-eases. You can begin to unravel the cause and heal these areas of your life. To heal is defined as to restore to health—to set aright, and to become whole and sound. Because we are made in the Image of Perfection, we already have the essence of that

Image to become whole and sound. We simply need to bring that essence into everyday living. Our Dis-eases point to the laws of the Image that are being developed. Thus, we can remove all guilt and questioning from our mind of having done "something" wrong. These prayers have been proven to be effective, and I can attest to positive results after practicing some variation of these prayers for over 50 years.

Look for a change in your perspective of the situation by practicing these prayers. Scientists have proven that energy follows thought. And as we speak, Universal Law responds to the words to change the situation. The power is within the words. An unwanted situation is often an accumulation of many FITs that have not been resolved. Your willingness to face your FITs about people, places, and things allows for the free flow of the development of the Image to take place. The power is within the words. The action is automatic. We simply need to say the words and look for a change.

It has been proven that in order to erase or heal a discordant thought, one of error, we must put in its place a word that is the opposite of the ones we are thinking. These prayers have been designed to correct the error thoughts by using opposite ones to bring the Power of corrected thoughts into your life.

Use whatever prayer is closest to the Law of Mind, Soul or Body for your case. If it is not exactly right for you, the words you need will come to you. The prayers will help you to connect with your Spirit and bridge the gap between your Mind, Soul, and Spirit (or body, soul and spirit).

It is suggested that you read the laws across the page from left to right from the Universal Laws chart in order to determine what faculty is in development. For example, if you are feeling fearful, read the prayer entitled "Fear" until your fear subsides. Some Laws of Spirit are repeated in healing or restoring the mind and soul as there are only seven Laws governing the Spirit to our present knowledge. Our feelings, images, and thoughts are the only yardsticks to measure how effectively we operate in this world.

Alma M. Stevens

September 2015

Introduction

Heretofore, we have recognized the body and its function and have a good foundation of what the body's needs are, i.e., nourishment, movement, sanitation, rest, etc. We govern ourselves accordingly. Similarly, we recognize the physical laws that govern traffic patterns, knowing that when they are disobeyed, there is a consequence. We recognize and respect the laws of gravity and electricity; we obey them, knowing that they have consequences as well.

These are examples of Universal Laws, which we cannot bend or break. As it relates to the body, Universal Law is an automatic process that quickens the Image in which we are made and supersedes all physical, emotional, mental, and spiritual states of the Whole Person. So it is with the Mind, Soul, and Spirit, as these are aspects or parts of the Image in which we are made.

We call the Physical State the Body in this writing. It is the way we feel at the moment that brings about the event, illness, or condition we experience. The Soul is part of the Image in which we are made; it holds that part of the Whole Person that is undeveloped in the Image. The Mental State is what we are consciously or unconsciously thinking, and it informs how we create our feelings. The Spiritual State or Law is the part of the Whole Person that is being developed. Our mind is the director – how we think. It has been proven that we cannot change an event, dis-ease, or condition if we do not change the way we are thinking. Our thoughts lead us to think.

The prayers in this book are a method to activate the changes necessary to release the experiences we do not want and become receptive to the experiences we do want. The changes in thought must be followed by taking action. Since, as individuals, we decide how we feel, what we imagine, and what we think, we can decide at any time to change the feelings, images, or thoughts we hold.

Many people struggle with their feelings, images, and thoughts and have never been taught to identify the difference between them. For example, we are often asked how we feel, and our answer for the most part is, "I feel fine." If only you knew the truth about who you really are! You are not your body. You are not your Soul. And you are not your mind. You are more than you can imagine. You were made in the Image of Perfection! Therefore, your answer should be, "I feel enthusiastic! I feel marvelous! I feel awesome!" These words more accurately describe your identity as one who is made in the Image of Perfection. The definition we are selecting to describe the Image in which we are made is "lacking nothing essential to the whole; complete of its nature of kind."

When we take responsibility for what we feel, what we imagine, and what we think, we live a more peaceful life. I invite you to use the prayers in *Heal Your Mind and Your Body Will Heal* to aid you in understanding the difference between who you really are and who you think you are. The prayers, though subtle, will affect a change just by repeating them, as that is one way of learning. The power is within the words. Spend time reading them twice a day and prepare to be transformed.

Instruction for Use of Prayers

Review the prayers and determine the one with the most charge around your FIT. I suggest that you work on one dis-ease at a time until you experience a difference in your FITs. Read the prayer until you feel differently about the same thing. Because most of us cannot separate our FITs, we call them one thing when, in reality, they are something else.

For example, we may judge a feeling as jealousy (feeling that something is being taken away from us), when it is really envy. When we practice reading the prayer for jealousy, it will become clear to us that we are really feeling envious (coveting someone else's possessions or qualities).

Every feeling, image, or thought you entertain, is developing or retarding the expression of the Image in which you are made. Every experience you have ever had, regardless of how you have judged it, was and is necessary in the developing the Image in which you were made.

All experiences of Mind, Soul, and Spirit are to enable you to live beyond your feelings, images, and thoughts. However, you must first become aware of what you are feeling, imagining, and thinking before you can move beyond them. Our goal is to live from the Image in which we are made. These prayers are not a panacea for life. They do not replace any medical diagnosis. However, they will enable you to handle your life with more peace and power. Peace and power come from the harmony of your feelings, images, and thoughts.

These prayers help to empower your entire being as you are uncovering the essence of the Image of Perfection in which you were made. You may or may not realize immediate results. However, I urge you to continue with the prayers until you see the changes you desire.

Universal Laws

MIND	SOUL	SPIRIT	EXPERIENCE
Anger	Patience	Peace	Repose
Criticism	Sympathy	Beauty	Splendor
Envy	Non-Interference	Life	Aliveness
Fear	Faith	Power	Mastery
Greed	Kindness	Joy	Ecstasy
Hate	Tolerance	Love	Transport
Hypocrisy	Courage	Power	Mastery
Jealousy	Duty	Life	Aliveness
Prejudice	Forgiveness	Peace	Repose
Selfishness	Generosity	Power	Mastery
Vanity	Aspiration	Wisdom	Knowing
Worry	Hope	Peace	Repose

(From Dr. Raymond Fleet's *Bringers of the Dawn*)

The next section of this book contains the definitions for each of the above words from the *American Heritage Dictionary* to help you sort out yours feelings, images, and thoughts. Our lives are made simple when we understand the purpose of what we are feeling, imagining, and saying. This is empowerment!

Definitions

LAWS OF MIND

Anger	A strong feeling of displeasure.
Criticism	The art of evaluating or analyzing with knowledge and propriety.
Envy	Resentful awareness of an advantage enjoyed by another joined with a desire to possess the same advantage.
Faith	Belief and trust; complete confidence.
Fear	A feeling of alarm or disquiet caused by the expectation of danger.
Forgiveness	To give love to; grant pardon without harboring resentment.
Generosity	Liberality or willingness in giving.
Greed	Excessive or reprehensible acquisitiveness.
Hate	To have a strong aversion.
Hope	Trust, reliance.
Jealousy	Disposed to suspect rivalry or unfaithfulness.
Kindness	Humane, tolerant, benevolent, charitableness.
Non-Interference	Refusal to impede, hinder, or intervene in the affairs of others.
Patience	The capacity of calm endurance.
Selfishness	Concerned excessively with oneself.
Sympathy	A feeling of loyalty, devotion, allegiance.
Tolerance	To endure without enmity.
Vanity	Quality of being empty or valueless.
Worry	To progress slowly by unceasing effort, despite troubles.

LAWS OF SOUL

Aspiration A strong desire for high achievement.

Courage The quality of mind or spirit that enables one to face danger with self-possession; valor.

Duty An act or a course of action that is expected of one.

LAWS OF SPIRIT

Beauty A pleasing quality associated with harmony.

Joy A condition or feeling of high pleasure or delight.

Life A spiritual state regarded as a transcending of death.

Love A strong fondness or enthusiasm for something.

Peace The absence of war. A state of tranquility.

Power The capacity to act or perform effectively.

Wisdom Understanding of what is true, wise.

BEYOND LAW (EXPERIENCE)

Alive In existence or active.

Ecstasy A state of exalted delight in which normal understanding is felt to surpass.

Knowing Suggestive of secret or private information; completely understood.

Mastery Possession of consummate skill: dominion.

Repose The state of being at rest. Tranquility.

Splendor Brilliance; great light or luster; grandeur.

Transport To move to strong emotions; enrapture; carry away.

Physical State: Body/Dis-ease   Abdomen
Emotional State: Soul – trust, harmony, self-worth
Mental State: Mind – worry, judgment, anxiety
Spiritual State: Law – Wisdom (undeveloped)

I surrender to the Image of Perfection in which I am made. I am modest in my assessment of who I am. I trust who I am and I am in harmony with that Image. I refuse to believe thoughts of worry, judgment, and anxiety as necessary for me to express Divine Wisdom. I accept thoughts of peace, decision, and relief to move through this experience. I embrace thoughts of trust, harmony, and value to express Divine Wisdom. My feelings, images, and thoughts are my guideposts to receive Divine Wisdom. I am worthy to receive. I am open to receive. I court thoughts that are commendable, compatible, and consistent with the Image in which I am made. I am ethical and trustworthy in my assessment of my life. I am important to this world and approach my life in a simple manner, praising who I am. I am unpretentious in my judgment of who I am. I bring forth the dignity of who I am. I do not underestimate my ability to heal my feelings, images, and thoughts. I embrace thoughts of worthiness, submissive only to feelings of joy. I praise my feelings. I use my feelings to bring out the gentleness within the Image in which I am made. I approve of myself just the way I am. I am made in the Image of Perfection. I now bring my thoughts back to the truth of who I am and commend myself for my willingness to heal my feelings, images, and thoughts. I am successful. I am effective. I am useful. I draw upon my understanding of the Image in which I am made to bring forth the essence of Divine Wisdom. My understanding is sound. My thoughts are elevated. My perception is keen. I discern the truth of me through this experience, and I am grateful. I am Divine Wisdom. I am thankful for this opportunity to express Divine Joy, and for this truth about who I am.

Physical State: Body/Dis-ease/Appearance   Abscess
Emotional State: Soul – Forgiveness, release
Mental State: Mind – stagnation, inertia, listlessness
Spiritual State: Law – Joy (undeveloped)

In this moment, I give myself unstintingly to Life spontaneously and with joy. The more I seek, the more I shall find. I set myself and all others free to express Divine Joy as I forgive myself. I am courageous in my ability to express Divine Joy. Therefore, I refute thoughts of stagnation, inertness, and listlessness. I maintain to be true that I am active, dynamic, and energetic. I command of myself to enjoy this opportunity to express Divine Joy. Pleasure, delight, and ecstasy compliment my world. I am free to feel, imagine, and think thoughts that soothe and alleviate the pressure to express Divine Joy. I take time to appreciate the majesty and splendor of Life and accept only good as my divine right. I am involved with the totality of Life. Joyfully, I accept the fullness of life. I seek and find happiness in every experience. This experience is for my highest good, and I accept it as so. I forgive myself and all others. I release and let go all that does not serve me. I see myself as I truly am. I unify my feelings, images, and thoughts, and tap into the wellspring of Divine joy. All desires, attitudes, and needs reflect the fulfillment of Divine Joy. I am of good cheer as I accept that I am made in the Image and likeness of my Creator. I praise everyone and everything. I unify with all life in Joy. I revel in joyous activities. I participate in activities that bring laughter and fun. I trust the Image in which I am made. I move with lightness of feet. I move swiftly from activity to activity to create Divine Joy in my life. I sing songs of praise for my feelings, images, and thoughts. I am filled with joy, and I am cheerful in my attitude towards life. I am gentle with myself in assessing my feelings, images, and thoughts. I am thankful for the gift of Life and for my capacity and ability to receive Divine Joy.

Physical State: Body/Dis-ease/Appearance   Accidents
Emotional State: Soul – Purpose, rest, tranquility
Mental State: Mind – stressed, burdened, aimless
Spiritual State: Law – Peace (undeveloped)

Right now, I move into a world of Peace. I live in a world of peace. Peace is at the center of my mind. I know that my true dwelling place is in the world of Peace. Therefore, I order my thoughts to declare untrue the appearance of stress, burdens, and aimlessness as necessary to express Divine Peace. I affirm positively that my Purpose is Divine. Rest and tranquility are necessary to experience Divine Peace. I court thoughts of value, worth, and significance, which free me. I am at ease. I organize my world according to my purpose. I am consistent as I discern my images, feelings, and thoughts. I affirm equanimity, poise, and self-confidence as the order of my feelings, images, and thoughts. I am quiet, still, and at rest. I order my world of thought to think thoughts of security. I command myself to be at ease. I rest in sweet repose. I allow Divine Peace to come into my world. I stand firm and embrace feelings, images, and thoughts of harmony, unity, and concordance from the Image of Perfection in which I am made. I become still as I accept my feelings, images, and thoughts as a guide to participate in life. I take charge of my thoughts, and I dwell in a world of Peace. I am still. I am calm. I rest in the silence of Peace in my world. I draw upon good judgment and insight for what I need to know and understand. My world is now filled with Divine Peace. I see the Presence and the Power of good in all my feelings, images, and thoughts. I now trust that which flows through me as good and very good. I am calm and patient with my feelings, images, and thoughts to express Divine Peace. Divine Peace is my birthright, and I draw upon my inheritance to move through this and all events in my life. I am the Light in my world, and I allow myself the privilege of shining. I give thanks for clear thinking and a peaceful heart. It is done.

Physical State: Body/Dis-ease/Appearance   Aches
Emotional State: Soul – unity, balance, courage
Mental State: Mind – separation, unloved
Spiritual State: Law – Joy (undeveloped)

I find pleasure in entertaining ideas of joy and fun things to do. Everything I need to support me in my desire to express joy is within my feelings, images, and thoughts. I am aware of my oneness with all life, and I am part of it. I participate in Life. As Divine Joy is a gift of life, I accept this Divine gift and draw upon it for my happiness. I refuse to indulge in thoughts of separation and frustration. I accept all feelings, images, and thoughts of unity, love, and encouragement as my way of being. I am in perfect and divine accord with my life. I am conscious that there is complete unity in life. Divine order is established in my feelings, images, and thoughts to express that unity. I take delight in discerning my direction in bringing forth Divine Joy. I accept joy and happiness at all times. I give freely and joyfully to Life, and I receive from Life all that makes me joyful and happy. In this moment, I seek my union with Life. I withdraw the veils that hide my true nature and thereby unveil the Reality of my life. I allow my inward nature to penetrate all feelings, images, and thoughts and uncover Divine Joy. Happiness increases my capacity for love. My appreciation of Life's gifts expands. I welcome every opportunity to discover Divine Joy. I now enter into the fullness of the Joy that is mine. I trust my feelings, images, and thoughts to bring forth Divine Joy. Joy confirms my faith. I participate in fun activities to bring joy into my life. Joy fills my life. Joy dominates my mood. I open up my life to accept Divine Joy as it flows through me in this experience. I am cheerful. I have a deep sense of inner calm. I desire to express joy and exhibit strength, peace, and beauty. I do what is before me in gladness and in joy. With a grateful heart, I am now filled with joy.

Physical State: Body/Dis-ease   Adrenal Glands
Emotional State: Soul – Loyalty, perseverance, steadfastness
Mental State: Mind – anxious, burdened, hopeless
Spiritual State: Law – Power (undeveloped)

I now turn to that which I know is real within me and assure myself of the Image of Perfection in which I am made. I remain steadfast, trustworthy, and reliable in my determination to express Divine Power. I am loyal as I persevere for my right to express Divine Power. I am devoted to uncovering my feelings, images, and thoughts to express Divine Power. I now refuse anxious thoughts, burdens, and defeat as an option. I accept only thoughts that relieve my mind and allow ease and freedom to circulate in my world. I am successful, confident, and assured of my ability to govern my world. I am calm and peaceful. My faith sustains my expectancy at all time. My ability to express Divine Power depends upon my acceptance and my expectancy. I have faith in the power that is within me. I have confidence in me. I trust the Power and conviction of truth. I tell myself the truth and stand unmovable upon that truth. I become single-minded and direct my feelings, images, and thoughts towards the truth of me. I rejoice in receiving wisdom and understanding of who I am and fully accept Divine Power as it flows through me. I claim the victory over my thoughts and express Divine Power. Everything I do prospers. I expect only good. My feelings, images, and thoughts guide me in my expression of Divine Power, and I face life squarely. I dip into the wellspring of fortitude within me. I see clearly, and I think with precision and forethought. I move in fidelity. I now move in trust, standing firm, knowing that only good can come to me through my faith in Divine Power. I demonstrate the truth of my Being. I have the tenacity to overcome any and all events to express Divine Power. I now take dominion over all my thoughts. With a heart filled with gratitude, I let it go.

Physical State: Body/Dis-ease/Appearance   AIDS
Emotional State: Soul — tranquility, harmony, concord
Mental State: Mind — angry, unloved, hopeless
Spiritual State: Law — Peace (undeveloped)

I accept all that I need for ideas, inspiration, and guidance. I rely upon the Image in which I am made to guide me through this event, and whatever I have needed has already been provided. I accept my good now. I value my freedom to express Divine Peace. I release this and all experiences to the Image of Perfection in which I am made. I let go. I surrender. I now order my world of thought and dwell upon thoughts that are tranquil, harmonious, and friendly. I embrace feelings of serenity, images that are optimistic, and thoughts of hope. I refuse to dwell upon thoughts of anger, of being unloved, and of hopelessness. I accept and dwell upon thoughts of forgiveness, knowing that I am loved by the Image in which I am made. I expect comfort, serenity, and ease. I am calm, peaceful, and at ease. I remove all judgment from my feelings, images, and thoughts and allow Divine Peace to flood my Being. I feel tranquil. I bring out the essence of joy in every thought. I take delight in uncovering my feelings, images, and thoughts and welcome thoughts that heal false ideas. Thoughts of the Image of Perfection in which I am made refresh me. I am soothed and nurtured by my feelings, images, and thoughts. I call them good and very good. I forgive myself and all others for mistaken ideas of who I am. I love myself. I am pleased. I now restore my world to Divine Peace. I am at ease. I stand ready to experience Divine Peace through my feelings, images, and thoughts. I am quiet. I am tranquil. Appearances are not real; therefore, I move beyond this appearance to the Reality of the Image of Perfection in which I am made. I am assured by that Image of who I am and of my Divine Purpose. I rest in sweet repose. I am grateful for this realization of the Truth about my true nature.

Physical State: Body/Dis-ease/Appearance Alcoholism
Emotional State: Soul — trust, reliance, fidelity
Mental State: Mind — guilty, inadequate, futile
Spiritual State: Law — Power (undeveloped)

I give myself completely to Life. I trust the Image in which I am made, relying upon the Power that is within that Image. I move forward, undaunted in my efforts to express Divine Power. I refuse to believe that the experience of alcoholism is necessary for me to express Divine Power. I renounce thoughts of guilt, inadequacy, and futility, and embrace thoughts of nobility, self-respect, and trust. I embrace thoughts of integrity, honor, and truth. I now trust the Image in which I am made to support me in my quest to express Divine Power. I stand upon my conviction of truth. I pledge loyalty and allegiance to bring forth the power that is within me. I dwell upon those attributes that bring me in harmony with my feelings, images, and thoughts. There are no useless thoughts. My feelings, images, and thoughts are my guideposts to receive Divine Power, and I do so now. I am effective, fruitful, and worthy to receive Divine Power. I am important to this world. I am sincere and honor my feelings, images, and thoughts. I now choose to be true to the best that is in me. Divine Power is my birthright. I am constantly aware of my inner promptings to experience Divine Power. I joyfully anticipate the experience of receiving Divine Power. My happiness increases my capacity to receive Divine Power. I welcome this opportunity to uncover my feelings, images, and thoughts to express Divine Power. I face Life squarely. I approve of myself. I give myself credit in telling the truth about me. I am honest in my assessment of my feelings, images, and thoughts. I withstand this and all experiences without bending. I have endurance, and I call it forth right now to support me in my desire to express Divine Power. I give thanks for uncovering the truth about me.

Physical State: Body/Affairs/Appearance   Aliveness (lack of)
Emotional State: Soul – Vital, vigorous, spirited
Mental State: Mind – aware, alert, awake
Spiritual State: Law – Joy (undeveloped)

I am filled with Joy. I am filled with Life. I feel alive. I exist in the Image in which I am made. I am not my body, I am not my mind, and I am not my soul. I am Spirit, made in the Image and Likeness of Perfection with the capacity to create my life and fulfill my purpose as a Spiritual Being. I take great delight in realizing the Image in which I am made. I am free to express Divine Joy in all my activities. I am conscious of my life. I am enlightened by the Image in which I am made. I am observant, tentative, and mindful of how I feel, what I say, and what I think. I am filled with Divine Joy. I am energetic, bold, and fearless. I face life with zest and enthusiasm. I observe nature, and I am filled with Joy. I am mindful of my feelings, images, and thoughts. They are my guide to inform me of my true nature as made in the Image and Likeness of Perfection. I am courageous and filled with vim, vigor, and vitality. I seize this opportunity to express Divine Joy. I am aware, alert, and awake. I am inspired daily as I move through all experiences with Joy in my heart. I love myself and praise myself for who I am. I now choose to live from the Image in which I am made. I am motivated by the beauty of Life. I participate in Life. I embrace life with confidence, cooperation, and compulsion. I rely upon my feelings, images, and thoughts to guide me through this experience. I face Life with bold assurance, self-reliance, and a willingness to live from the Image in which I am made. I engage in fun activities to express pleasure and delight. I am now filled with the joy of Life to express my true nature. I trust who I am. I love who I am and what I aspire to accomplish in life. I am free to give thanks.

Physical State: Body/Dis-ease/Appearance   Anemia
Emotional State: Soul – devotion, order, faith
Mental State: Mind – angry, possessive, inconsistent
Spiritual State: Law – Joy (undeveloped)

I see well in perfecting the Kingdom of Joy within me. I now see perfection in all creation and the beauty of the Image in which I am made. I am filled with the essence of that Image; therefore, joy overflows into my life. I am devoted to bringing joy into my feelings, images, and thoughts. I refute the experience of anemia as real as I accept devotion to my life, order in my affairs, and faith in all my activities. I no longer think thoughts that are angry, possessive, and inconsistent. I now embrace, court, and dwell upon loving and truthful thoughts. I release all feelings, images, and thoughts that are not consistent with my purpose to express Divine Joy. I bring order to my life now. I am reliable, loyal, and trustworthy. I honor my feelings, images, and thoughts. I am good natured and gratified. I rejoice in this opportunity to express Divine Joy in my world. I am pleased. I have confidence and certitude as I rely solely on my images, feelings, and thoughts to guide me through this experience. I rejoice in expressing each thought in happiness and awe. I am free to face life in the Image in which I am made. Joy and ecstasy radiate throughout my world. I am filled with joy. I experience this life in joy and harmony. Love fills my life. Joy fills my being. I am at peace with who and what I am. I am the joy of my life. I am true to my Divine nature. I am free and at ease as I permit only feelings of joy to flood my being. I love myself for who I am. I am grateful for the uncovering of this truth. It is done.

Physical State: Body Affairs/Dis-ease/Appearance   Anger
Emotional State: Soul – love, approval, acceptance
Mental State: Mind – anguish, hostility, discord
Spiritual State: Law – Love/Peace (undeveloped)

I consciously enter a world of peace. I allow peace to come into my world. I am made in the Image of Perfection, and as such, I now claim my birthright to speak words of truth to heal my world of affairs. I refuse the appearance of anger as necessary to experience Divine Love and Divine Peace. I state that I am loving, calm, and peaceful. I refuse to believe thoughts of anguish, hostility, and discord as necessary to fulfill my desire to express Divine Love and Peace. I embrace thoughts of comfort, amicability, and harmony to move through this experience. I remove all judgment from my feelings and thoughts. I have everything within me to satisfy all desire, and I embrace feelings of joy. I think only thoughts that are peaceful. I am calm. I allow the wisdom in my feelings, images, and thoughts to pervade my life. I am satisfied with who I am. I love who I am. I praise who I am. I stand firm and embrace feelings of harmony, unity, and concordance with the Image in which I am made. I become still and accept all events in life as guides to my participation in life. I accept the peace that is beyond all understanding. I take charge of my thoughts and dwell in a world of Peace. I have evidence of stillness. I am tranquil, quiet, and content. I see the Presence and Power of good in all images, feelings, and thoughts. I now trust that which flows through me as good and very good. I am calm and patient in all my actions, feelings, and thoughts. The essence of Divine Peace flows though me, and I rest in sweet repose. I am serene and content with myself. I am undisturbed by outer circumstances and give thanks that it is done.

Physical State: Body/Dis-ease   Ankle
Emotional State: Soul – praise, virtue, truth
Mental State: Mind – hopeless, insecure, inflexible
Spiritual State Law – Power (undeveloped)

I keep my mind open and receptive to new ideas. I praise my feelings, images, and thoughts, as they are a guidepost to my experience of Divine Power. I include every part of my life in all my activities. I respect my feelings and now move through all judgments that I have placed upon them. I am honest in my assessment of the truth. I abstain from thoughts of hopelessness, insecurity, and inflexibility. I confirm, embrace, and dwell upon thoughts that are encouraging, expectant, and confident. I am secure in the Image in which I am made. I am flexible in thought and feelings. I am responsive to Life, and I move gently and easily. I have regard for my feelings, images, and thoughts. I allow Divine Wisdom to guide me to that part of me that supports right action in all that I do. I move gracefully through this experience with the understanding that I am uncovering the Image in which I am made. I have the capacity to be adaptable in all events. I am gentle with myself. I now seek change and move with sufficient strength to express Divine Power. I am encouraged in my efforts. I respect my feelings, images, and thoughts, and I express Divine Power. I move into integrity. I draw upon Divine Power. I step out boldly and freely, confident in my ability to know the truth. I accept and embrace feelings of assurance, confidence, and courage. I have the courage to move through this experience in love for myself and all others. I am true to myself. I love myself. I bless myself and all others. I search my feelings, images, and thoughts to know the truth about this situation, and I am made free. I am brave and strong. I am grateful for this experience, as all experiences lead me to the Image in which I am made. It is complete.

Physical State: Body/Affairs   Aspiration
Emotional State: Soul – endeavor, purpose, intention
Mental State: Mind – insufficiency, seeking, wishing
Spiritual State: Law – Wisdom (undeveloped)

In this moment, I am content with the knowledge of who I am. I seek Divine Wisdom in discovering who I am. I use foresight, prudence, and astuteness in making all decisions about my life. I am successful in all undertakings. I refute thoughts of insufficiency, seeking, and wishing. I accept thoughts of sufficiency and finding wisdom in all things. I no longer wish for anything outside of me. I know all that I need to know as I pursue my purpose to uncover the Image in which I am made. My intentions are honorable. I desire to share. I seek wisdom. I find wisdom. I allow the wisdom in my feelings to guide me to my highest desire. I expand my thought world to include Divine Wisdom. I have intelligence to cultivate Divine Wisdom. I have the mental capacity to embrace Divine Wisdom. I understand that my thoughts come to move me to a place in mind to develop Divine Wisdom. I rise in thought to who I am. I remove judgment from my feelings, images, and thoughts as I affirm with deep conviction that my feelings are my guide to live from the Image in which I am made. There is nothing outside of me to yearn for. I am content. I am guided and motivated by the Image in which I am made to conceive the purpose of every experience. I am vigilant in my desire to uncover my true feelings, images, and thoughts. Divine Wisdom is my gift, my inherent ability to know the Image in which I am made. I have the intelligence and foresight to know what I need to know whenever I need to know it. I rest in peace and with ease as I open up to receive Divine Wisdom. I give thanks for this realization, and it is done.

Physical State: Body/Affairs   Beauty
Emotional State: Soul – Inspiration, Illumination
Mental State: Mind – awe
Spiritual State: Law – Beauty (undeveloped)

I am made in the Image and Likeness of Perfection. I rise in thought to see the splendor in my feelings, images, and thoughts. I look through the eyes of beauty and see the symmetry of life. Beauty is in all things. I am agreeable, pleasant, and good-natured. I see life as flawless. I see my life increased, enhanced, and heightened by Divine Beauty. I look for beauty in all things; I see beauty in all forms. I remove judgment from my feelings, images, and thoughts to experience Divine Beauty. I am unified with ideas of beauty. I am illumined by the grandeur of Life. Divine beauty is my inheritance. My vision is clear. My life reflects the eternal truth of my creation. Beauty is everywhere. I trust my feelings, images, and thoughts to guide me in beholding the beauty of this earth. I see the magnificence of the earth. I am gentle with myself as beauty radiates from me. I see the exquisiteness of nature, and my heart leaps with joy. I am infused with Light. I take time to appreciate the majesty and beauty of Life and learn to live nobly in this world. Divine inspiration opens my eyes to an appreciation of the wonders of the Image in which I am made. I am involved in the totality of Life. I am renewed in body and mind as I joyfully accept the wholeness of the Divine Presence within me. I praise this moment, which gives me fullness of life, and I am thankful. I pause in thanksgiving for Divine Beauty. I see beauty in everything. I look through the eyes of praise, wisdom, and love to bring out the beauty that is inherent in all things. I am grateful for this knowledge, and it is done.

Physical State: Body/Dis-ease   Brain
Emotional State: Soul – harmony, tranquility
Mental State: Mind –anxious, tense, nervous
Spiritual State: Law – Peace (undeveloped)

As I identify with who I am, I become increasingly aware that I am made in the Image of Perfection, and I am divinely guided though this experience. I let go of struggle and move with confidence and assurance that my health is restored. I move with ease into a place where I am peaceful. My feelings, images, and thoughts are in harmony, and I become tranquil and still. I am now at peace. I refuse to entertain thoughts that are anxious, tense, or nervous, as I accept only thoughts that bring relief, relaxation, and tranquil feelings. I have the assurance from the Image in which I am made to experience Divine Peace. I bring equanimity into my world and balance my thinking. I am confident that I am restored to perfect health. I am in agreement and cooperation with my feelings, images, and thoughts to bring harmony and tranquility into my life. I am at Peace. I agree with all of life. I order my world to harmonize with my Divinity and adapt easily to experience Divine Peace. My life and experience grows into a vital, living, harmonious, and abundant expression of the Activity of Life. I accept peace. That which I accept in my mind is that which is actually mine. I am patient with myself. I let go of struggle and allow the essence of Divine Peace to flood my being. As I do so, there can only be right action taking place in my experience. I now identify myself completely with the energy and vitality of the Image in which I am made. I rest in sweet repose, and it is done.

Physical State: Body/Dis-ease   Breast
Emotional State: Soul – devotion, esteem, affinity
Mental State: Mind – disregard, deprivation
Spiritual State: Law – Love (undeveloped)

I begin by accepting myself unconditionally, just as I am. My self-acceptance is not dependent upon my physical appearance or the state of my worldly affairs. My acceptance depends upon the Image in which I am made. I am made from Love, and Love seeks only Its own fulfillment. Being all, nothing can be added to It, and nothing can be taken from It. It upholds, guides, and prospers all of my life. I am devoted to expressing Divine Love in my life, and I honor my tendency to develop Divine Love to govern my life. I refuse to disregard my feelings, images, and thoughts. I no longer ignore or deprive myself of love for myself and all others. I now accept and embrace loving thoughts in regard to my feelings, images, and thoughts. I heed these signposts as reminders of the Image in which I am made. I cultivate, strengthen, and sustain thoughts of love. I prepare my mind to accept only thoughts of love. I love myself, I honor myself, and I praise myself. All feelings have merit. I look for the increase in all feelings to express Divine Love. I gain from all feelings, images, and thoughts as I discern all emotion as profitable to bring forth vitality and Divine Joy. I am rewarded by my acceptance of the essence of Divine Love that flows through me. I release myself from all that no longer serves my commitment to dwell within the Image in which I am made. I have all that I need, and I express Divine Love in this experience. Love is all there is, and I claim that is what I am. I hold my thoughts in high esteem, giving each one consideration. I observe the screen of my mind to bring each thought to its highest potential. I surrender and offer each thought as a means of expressing Divine Love. I call each feeling, image, and thought good, and very good. In quiet confidence and praise, it is done.

Physical State: Body/Dis-ease/Appearance   Bruises
Emotional State: Soul – rapture, ardor, amity
Mental State: Mind – scattered, unsettled, disturbed
Spiritual State: Law – Love (undeveloped)

Every feeling, image, and thought emerges from the Image in which I am made. Ideas come with all the power that is necessary for completion and fulfillment. Right now, I identify with the Image in which I am made and take action upon my feelings, images, and thoughts to bring them into fullness. I trust that of which I am made. I desire to experience bliss, fervor, and understanding of this experience. I move with zeal, vigor, and enthusiasm. I refuse to believe in thoughts that are scattered, unsettled, and disturbed. I collect my thoughts and align my feelings and images with them. I am eager in my desire to express Divine Love. I look for and see beauty, love, and joy in this opportunity to express Divine Love. Feelings represent energy flowing through me, and I accept and direct that energy into constructive ventures. I remove all judgment from my feelings, as they support the Image in which I am made. I face life boldly, courageously, and daringly. I call all feelings good and very good. My union with my feelings gives me the courage to live from the Image in which I am made, and I draw upon the power of Divine Love for stability. I am gentle in assessing my feelings, and I place great worth upon myself. Divine Power now attracts me to Ideas of Divine Love. I dwell upon thoughts of ease. I cooperate with myself. I praise myself and every thought, as each one leads to my full potential. I carefully choose my thoughts, realizing that my thoughts express the truth about who I am. I seek the truth in each thought. The Law of Love responds in accordance with my realization and acceptance. I elevate my feelings, images, and thoughts with proper discrimination. I give thanks for who I am, and it is done.

Physical State: Body/Dis-ease/Appearance   Bunion
Emotional State: Soul – endurance, truth, pleasure
Mental State: Mind – fear, inflexibility, rigidity, anguish
Spiritual State: Law – Joy (undeveloped)

I rejoice in expressing all feelings, images, and thoughts. I accept life, and I am determined to express Divine Joy in all that I undertake. I have the stamina, permanence, and courage to move through all experiences. I seek the truth and find pleasure in uncovering the truth. Truth brings me Joy. I refuse to accept fear of moving forward, inflexibility in my actions, rigidity in my thought, and torment in my world as necessary. I accept, embrace, and court feelings that are daring, lighthearted, and comforting. I relax. I am at ease. I permit only feelings of joy to flood my being. I am undaunted in my resolve to express Divine Joy. Joy and ecstasy radiate from my being. I abstain from indulging in thoughts of anguish and torture as I indulge in thoughts that bring peace. I am spontaneous and free to express gladness and leisure in all my expressions. I experience life in joy and harmony. I represent the Image in which I am made; therefore, I take delight in this opportunity to express Divine Joy. I am the joy of my life. Love fills my life. Joy fills my being. I feel secure. I liberate myself from feelings of responsibility to anyone or anything other than the Image in which I am made. I become flexible in my thinking and my need to express life in Joy. I am honest and open. Channels of good flow in and through me freely and generously. I let go of the past and face the future filled with courage and Joy. I honor, respect, and support my feelings, images, and thoughts in order to express Divine Joy. I rejoice in expressing the Image in which I am made. I now claim Divine Joy as the power that governs my life. I give thanks as I accept this to be the truth about me, and it is finished.

Physical State: Body/Dis-ease/Appearance   Calluses
Emotional State: Soul – discernment, good judgment, acute
Mental State: Mind – folly, absurdity, irrational
Spiritual State: Law – Wisdom (undeveloped)

I now claim my gift of Wisdom as I seek to understand the Purpose of this experience. I open my mind, and with enthusiasm, I accept this experience and call it good and very good. I have the insight to discern what is before me. My assessment of my feelings, images, and thoughts are sound. I draw upon my intuition to guide me through this experience. I refuse to believe thoughts of folly, absurdity, and irrationality as necessary to express Divine Wisdom. I affirm and dwell upon prudent, sound, and wise thoughts. I am capable of good judgment to ascertain decisions that support the Image in which I am made. I observe Life and take intelligent and astute actions. I have a deep sense of inner calm, a complete faith in Divine Wisdom as it flows through me. I know the Truth and I am free. I use good judgment in making all decisions, which gives me clear directions to express Divine Wisdom. Wisdom is my divine gift, and I use my gift wisely in understanding all that is real and lasting. Everything I need to know is made known to me as Divine Wisdom. I recognize the guidance and the right direction for me to take upon all actions. I hear. I listen. I am guided in all my undertakings. I see Divine Guidance everywhere in the world about me. I am exacting, accurate, and virtuous in judging my obligations. I free my feelings, images, and thoughts to make wise decisions. I look for the divinity in all feelings, images, and thoughts, and peace comes into my world. I have a deep sense of inner calm, a complete faith in Divine Wisdom as it flows through me. In deepest gratitude and with a thankful heart, I let it be.

Physical State: Body/Dis-ease/Appearance   Cancer (any form)
Emotional State: Soul – verve, veracity, duration
Mental State: Mind – anger, despair, resentment
Spiritual State: Law – Love (undeveloped)

I free my feelings, images, and thoughts from fear and negative pursuits, thus remaining a perfect channel for the Image in which I am made. Daringly, I draw upon Divine Love to shine through my affairs. I evaluate my feelings, images, and thoughts with proper discrimination. I move with vigor, vitality, and endurance. I refuse to indulge in thoughts of anger, despair, and resentment. I accept, embrace, and dwell upon thoughts of love, hope, and approval. I respect myself. I love myself. I welcome thoughts of persistence, vitality, and enthusiasm. I am accepting of myself. I am alive with Divine Love. I forgive myself and all others. I expect and demand of myself to express Divine Love in all events. I now recognize the Image in which I am made and accept It as I am. My body has intelligence that does the thing necessary to put every organ in its right place. This Intelligence causes every organ of my body to perform its duty spontaneously and effectively, after the Image in which I am made. I now sense perfection within me. All evidence of dis-ease is now erased by the action of perfect organs, clean and pure in this moment. This is the truth about my body, and I know that truth right now. I am now conscious of and expect only absolute perfection in my body, mind, and soul. Perfect health is mine to enjoy. Knowing my body is the dwelling place for the Image in which I am made, I rise to that image right now. I remove all judgment upon my feelings, images, and thoughts. My health—my physical well being as well as my mental poise and peace—are drawn from the Image in which I am made. It is my Source of Perfection. The Law of that Image is the healing presence of Life, forever restoring my mind and body to its original perfection. I love myself. In quiet confidence and gratitude, I give thanks for perfect health.

Physical State: Body/Dis-ease/Appearance   Carpel Tunnel
Emotional State: Soul – faith, trust, reliance
Mental State: Mind – hopelessness, weakness, impotence
Spiritual State: Law – Power (undeveloped)

I sense the inner power within everything. I know this Power responds to me in love. I commune with this Power joyfully, and I am at rest. I receive accordingly. No one can take from me, and no one may give to me except that which I have accepted in my thinking. I now call upon my faith in the Image in which I am made and trust It to guide and direct me in all that I do. I rely upon my feelings, images, and thoughts as guideposts to receive Divine Power. I declare thoughts of hopelessness, weakness, and impotence as untrue in my world. I declare positively and firmly that only thoughts that are hopeful, promising, and encouraging are true expressions of the Image in which I am made. I am optimistic in my resolve to restore my world with Divine Power. I am strong and effectual. I have the potential to express Divine Power, and I take this opportunity to prove my ability to bring forth that potential. I reclaim my power. I am confident that I have the aptitude to express Divine Power. I view my feelings, images, and thoughts with justice. I am intelligent. My thinking is my contract with the Image in which I am made, and I now direct it into the patterns that I desire for my life. I remember who I am. I mentally reach out and use the Power within me wisely by opening up my mind to receive. I now deliberately raise my mind to unite with the Image in which I am made, and I claim my rightful heritage of my full supply. Here and now, I accept the whole gift of life. I am conscious of knowing what to do and am impelled to act intelligently upon every right impression. I rely upon the Law of the Image in which I am made. I am undaunted in my resolve to express Divine Power. I am grateful for the revelation of this truth about me, and it is done.

Physical State: Body/Dis-ease   Cardio Vascular
Emotional State: Soul – Harmony, Enthusiasm, Tranquility
Mental State: Mind – impatient, competitive, hostile
Spiritual State: Law – Divine Peace (undeveloped)

Divine Peace brings out my creativity, my self-giving, and my self-becoming. I now draw upon Divine Peace to aid in my discovery of the Image in which I am made. I am free to allow my true nature to come forward, and information is given to me to make way for Its passage through my feelings, images, and thoughts. That Image only knows Itself and Its Likeness. Peace, Power, and Wisdom are the basis upon which I stand to reveal the truth in this situation. Order, eagerness, and fervent feelings, images, and thoughts make an appearance in my life. I refuse to grant thoughts of impatience, competition, and hostility to govern my world of thought any longer. I ratify only thoughts of patience, cooperation, and agreement to infuse my world. I am in alliance with my feelings, images, and thoughts. Goodwill, amity, and congeniality pervade my mind to bring Divine Peace from the Image in which I am made. I am calm, peaceful, and serene in my assessment of my world. I am alive, alert, and aware of feelings that bring courage to meet all challenges in my daily affairs. I am at peace. Harmony radiates out through my world. I dwell upon superior and noble thoughts as they bring ideas out of Divine Peace. I take higher interest in all my feelings, images, and thoughts in order to receive Divine Peace. My perception is clear. As I call upon Divine Peace, It comes into full expression from the Image in which I am made. Peace prepares the foundation upon which I stand. Divine Peace stills all sense of discord. I seek friendship with all my feelings, images, and thoughts as they reveal companionship, brotherhood, and cheer. I discern all thoughts rightly as I acquaint myself with the Image of Perfection in which I am made. I resign myself to enjoy this opportunity to express Divine Peace. In thanksgiving and praise, it is complete.

Physical State: Body/Dis-ease   Chest
Emotional State: Soul – confidence, courage, assurance
Mental State: Mind – fear, insecurity, rejection
Spiritual State: Law – Divine Love (undeveloped)

I am now aware of Divine Love, and I vow to express It in all my feelings, images, and thoughts. I seek the power of love and bring it into my world. I am at liberty to feel all emotion as it comes from the Image in which I am made. It is my duty to release the essence of my Image through every feeling, image, and thought for the accomplishment of my Divine Purpose. Therefore, I call upon my innate storehouse of confidence, courage, and assurance to fill me with Divine Love. I abstain from thinking thoughts of fear, insecurity, and rejection as I make firm in my mind thoughts of faith, security, and acceptance. I am daring in my assessment of my world and rely upon the Image in which I am made. I honor my feelings, images, and thoughts and bring forth the bravery that is within me. I am undaunted in my efforts to express Divine Love in my life. I have the endurance, the stamina, and the valor to move through this experience to express Divine Love. I am loved, cared for, and appreciated by all. I tell myself the truth. My feelings, images, and thoughts are of one accord. I am calm, peaceful, and I rest in sweet repose. I accept feelings of peace, freedom, and contentment in my life. I remove the judgment upon my feelings. I sense orderliness and feel secure in my assessment of my feelings, images, and thoughts. Feelings of hidden hurts and grief now come forward for me to love, forgive, and to bless. I now know the Truth. I am made in the Image of Perfection, and my body is the channel to carry out that Perfection. I am undisturbed in my efforts to radiate Divine Love. I grasp life with enthusiasm. I embrace my feelings with tenderness, kindness, and fondness. I joyously move into life with zeal and enthusiasm. I accept Divine Love and give thanks in quiet confidence.

Physical State: Body/Dis-ease/Appearance   Cholesterol (high or low)
Emotional State: Soul – ecstasy, exhilaration, rapture
Mental State: Mind – despair, grief, sadness
Spiritual State: Law – Joy (undeveloped)

I sit in silent communion with my soul as I seek to feel Divine Joy. I feel capable of taking the initiative in shaping the kind and scope of life I desire for myself. I have a sense of more than adequate talent, ability, and an urge to use it. I lift my mind to receive bliss, vivacity, and felicity, and I express Divine Joy. Therefore, I refuse to believe that thoughts of despair, grief, and sadness are necessary for me. I affirm, embrace, and court feelings of delight, comfort, and cheer. I participate in activities that bring me happiness. An awareness of my inner power and capability rises up within me, and I know that I am equal to any demands made upon me. There is validity in my self-confidence, for it is the Image in which I am made. It is my True Nature, and I rise to my true nature right now. I now command an opportunity to express Divine Joy. As I speak these words and know the truth about my health, Divine Joy floods my Being. The power is within the words I speak. I accept, assert, and call upon all feelings of joy to spring out from the very depth of the Image in which I am made. I accept as real all feelings of pleasure and glee. My spirit soars. I allow Divine Joy to flow unobstructed through me to the nations of the world. I resolutely claim confidence, self-reliance, and determination to live life fully in joy and love. Divine Joy sustains me in all that I do. I am filled with Joy and welcome opportunities to express Divine Joy in all that I do. I rejoice as I am lifted to feelings of ecstasy and elation. I rejoice as I move joyously and spontaneously into the Image in which I am made. I am gentle in my assessment of feelings, images, and thoughts. I now draw upon the source of my strength to express Divine Joy. Divine Joy is complete, and it is the fulfillment of the law of my life. And I accept this as the Truth.

Physical State: Body/Dis-ease   Circulatory System
Emotional State: Soul – Conviction, discernment
Mental State: Mind – judgment, non-acceptance, burden
Spiritual State: Law – Love (undeveloped)

Daringly, I draw upon love to fill my body. I evaluate my feelings, images, and thoughts with proper discrimination. I move with valor into life, unfettered and unafraid. I am earnest in my quest to move into the Image in which I am made. I am free to love. I refuse to indulge in thoughts of judgment, non-acceptance, and burdens. Instead, I heal my body by accepting thoughts of discretion, encouragement, and hope. I view this experience as one that leads me to live in the Image in which I am made. I am aware of the need to love, and I change my perception to welcome thoughts of praise, adulation, and love. I regard the Image of who I am with tenderness, fondness, and adoration. I am one with that Image. The radiance from my light makes that which I choose to do for all people more acceptable, as all my actions are laced with love. I am aware of my unity with all life. What I am opens doors of opportunity before me and determines the measure of both my giving and receiving. I now open up to receive Divine Love, as it is my heritage. I was made from love. Divine Love sustains me in all that I feel, imagine, and think. Love is the way I choose. I draw upon joyful thoughts to create my world and to heal my body. Love attracts my good to me, and I gladly receive. Divine Love surrounds me. I trust myself; I love myself just as I am. I take action upon my feelings, images, and thoughts and bring them in harmony with who I know myself to be. I tell myself the truth. My appraisal of that which I am is demonstrated in my actions through my feelings, images, and thoughts. What I know, I become. I am in my true place, living from the Image in which I am made. I see myself as I truly am. I am thankful for the healing of my body, soul, and mind.

Physical State: Body/Dis-ease/Appearance   Common Cold
Emotional State: Soul – enlightenment, clarity, order
Mental State: Mind – confusion, resentment, chaos
Spiritual State: Law – Peace (undeveloped)

I now relax and allow peace to flow though me. I bring forward that which is clear, loving, and calm. I open up to receive enlightenment, clarity, and order in my life, and I express the Image in which I am made. I am at rest. I refuse to dwell upon thoughts of confusion, resentment, and chaos. I dwell upon thoughts that are quiet, appropriate, and calming. My mind is illumined, transparent, and composed as I express Divine Peace. I rest in sweet repose. My feelings, images, and thoughts are guideposts to advise and inform me of the Image in which I am made. I turn to calm feelings, serene images, and peaceful thoughts. I am tranquil and still. I hold my feelings, images, and thoughts in high regard, and I approve of all things. Harmony, fellowship, and friendship are now set forth to guide all my feelings, images, and thoughts. Any seeming imperfection is now transformed into the perfect idea of my true self. Even though I have misunderstood my union with all Life, there is no judgment against me from the Image in which I am made. I harbor no unkind thought. I dwell on no unkind deed. My feelings allow me the openness, compatibility, and courtesy to express Divine Peace. I am unlimited in my ability to govern my life through my feelings, images, and thoughts. Light flows through my thoughts for acceptance. I find clarity of thought as I dwell upon thoughts that are in harmony with my being. With my mind quiet and composed, my actions are in order. I am calm. I am peaceful. I love myself. Right now, I allow my feelings, images, and thoughts to serve as reflections that pave the way for me to experience Divine Peace. I am still. I embrace my feelings as serviceable, beneficial, wholesome, and necessary to express the Life of the Image in which I am made. I draw upon the Image in which I am made to enlighten me so that I may know the purpose of this experience. I am in agreement with my feelings, images, and thoughts. I am grateful for the realization of the truth about this experience.

Physical State: Body/Affairs/Appearance   Courage (lack of)
Emotional State: Soul – fortitude, boldness, intrepidity
Mental State: Mind – terror, fear, dread
Spiritual State: Law – Power (undeveloped)

I know that love protects and guards me, and that I am guided to pathways of peace and security. I am filled with confidence. I am brave in my actions. All fear is removed from my feelings, images, and thoughts as I move with certainty of speech and action. I live in expectation of an enthusiastic and joy-filled life. I remain steadfast in my desire to develop Divine Power. I now still my mind to know that I am unified with my feelings, images, and thoughts. I refuse to believe that terror, fear, and dread are necessary to express Divine Power. I approve of thoughts of security, bravery, and confidence. I resolve all conflict between my purpose and personal expression. I gain strength of character. I have the physical stamina and spiritual fortitude to face all feelings, images, and thoughts. I develop the quality of mind to move with confidence through all experiences. I am fearless in all my undertakings. I am bold in understanding the Image in which I am made. I am fearless in my endeavors. I put my trust in the power that is within me. I have the ability to withstand without bending. This experience is to aid me in fulfilling my desire to express Divine Power. I welcome it. I rise above the sense of separation between my feelings, images, and thoughts. I call forth and claim my gift of courage. I am strong. I am sturdy in stature. My moments are filled with joyful activity, and my nights are filled with peace as Divine Power surges through me. I rest in peace as I face all feelings, images, and thoughts that come to teach me to use my inherent power. I give thanks for this understanding.

Physical State: Body/Affairs/Appearance   Criticism
Emotional State: Soul – compliment, praise, commend
Mental State: Mind – disapprove, reproach, censure
Spiritual State: Law – Beauty (undeveloped)

I now look at life through the eyes of beauty. I find no fault in my world. I regard and respect the Image in which I am made. I am whole, perfect, and complete. I have the essence of the Image in which I am made, and I express Divine Beauty. I commend myself for all my creations. I praise my feelings, images, and thoughts, as this is my path to uncover the Image in which I am made. I refuse to believe thoughts of disapproval, reproach, and censure as necessary for me to receive the essence of Divine Beauty. I embrace thoughts of approval and praise. I laude my feelings, images, and thought as I realize the Image in which I am made. I have all the love, wisdom, and power I need in this moment. I face any situation that confronts me, and I handle every situation easily and successfully. I praise every situation, using discrimination in assessing every feeling, image, and thought. I give joyous thanks for my work, my friends, my co-workers, my family and the duties that make up the hours of the passing day. Truth comes from love. I commend myself for my ability to discern my feelings and accept them as real and natural. I let go of my opinion of facts and see the truth. I inquire of my feelings to guide me in this experience. I praise, laude, and approve of all feelings as I am exonerated. My feelings are channels for expressing my Divinity. I absolve myself of all mistaken feelings. I am competent, qualified, and have the capacity to bring all thoughts of criticism into harmony with my Divine Purpose. I take leadership over all feelings, images, and thoughts. I commit myself to living from the Image in which I am made. I give thanks for this experience.

Physical State: Body/Dis-ease/Appearance   Cysts
Emotional State: Soul — rapture, exultation
Mental State: sadness, melancholy, contrition
Spiritual State: Law — Joy (undeveloped)

As I allow my feelings, images, and thoughts to guide me to activities of Joy, I become increasingly aware of who I am. I am unified with life. I know my purpose is to express the Image in which I am made through transparency. States of rapture and exultation are natural states for me to experience here and now. Therefore, I let go of sadness, melancholy, and contrite thoughts, and I embrace thoughts that are cheerful, delightful, and uplifting. I take pleasure in assessing my feelings, images, and thoughts so that I may receive Divine Joy. I am delighted to participate in my life— to live from the Image in which I am made. I now know my true nature is of good. My life and experiences grow into a vital, living, harmonious, and abundant expression of the Activity of the Image in which I am made. That Image is Perfect. I am perfect. I agree with all feelings, images, and thoughts, as they are my guideposts to the Image in which I am made. I am patient with myself. I love myself. I am in cooperation with life. I govern my feelings, images, and thoughts to conform with who I am—made in the Image and likeness of Perfection. I order my world to harmonize with my Divinity. I adapt easily to experience Divine Joy. I embrace feelings of Joy. I am gay, cheerful, and merry in expressing Divine Joy. The essence of Joy floods my being. I harbor thoughts of joy. I go forth with purpose, vitality, and self-confidence, sensing Divine Joy with every breath I take. I pledge joy as the loadstone of my life, the great and supreme Reality. I am created out of Divine Love and Divine Joy. I am grateful for this realization and vow to bring Divine Joy into my life, aided by Divine Love. I welcome each feeling, image, and thought. I move forward in Divine Love.

Physical State: Body/Dis-ease/Appearance　　Dementia
Emotional State: Soul – trust, faith, belief
Mental State: Mind – hopelessness, struggle, anger
Spiritual State: Law – Power (undeveloped)

I remain firm in my conviction that I am made in the Image of Perfection, and I am sustained and strengthened by that Image. I rely upon my inner power and wisdom to lead, guide, and direct me into actions that restore my ability to express Divine Power. I am fortified in the knowledge that the Good that is mine for the asking awaits me. I meet each challenge with confidence and satisfaction. I trust who I am and have faith and belief that this experience has come to pass. I refute thoughts of hopelessness, struggle, and anger as necessary to express Divine Power. I accept and embrace thoughts that encourage hope and optimism. Thoughts of surrender to express Divine Power now envelop my world. I am free to trust my feelings, images, and thoughts, as they reflect to me that which I need to express from the Image in which I am made. It is my duty to express Divine Power in my world, and I am reassured by my faith with a certainty that I am capable. I have confidence in my feelings, images, and thoughts to guide me through this experience. I am composed and quiet as I receive thoughts that aid in fulfilling my desire to express Divine Power. I express the Wholeness of life in this experience, and I am in perfect agreement with my feelings, images, and thoughts. I now accept all situations as supportive of my experience in my world. I attract that which I desire to be included in my experience by agreeing with it. Before I speak, my good is established. I live constantly in the midst of good as Divine Power flows through me. I am showered with blessings and receive them graciously and gratefully. I praise who I am. My belief is now stabilized in the Image in which I am made. I entertain thoughts that are in cooperation with my true nature. I accept peace, gratitude, and courage. I give thanks that my world is restored to receive Divine Power.

Physical State: Body/Dis-ease/Appearance   Depression
Emotional State: Soul – exaltation, pleasure, rapture
Mental State: Mind – dejected, desolate
Spiritual State: Law – Joy (undeveloped)

This day, I sit in silent communion with my soul as I seek to express Divine Joy. I lift my feelings, images, and thoughts to express pleasure and rapture. I refuse to entertain thoughts of dejection and desolation. I embrace and court thoughts that are elated and cultivate thoughts of praise. I am not alone. I nourish my feelings, images, and thoughts to express Divine Joy. This experience is one that leads me to the Image in which I am made. I seize this opportunity to express Divine Joy as it flows through me. I am loved, appreciated, and praised for who I am. I say no to all feelings of resistance and burdens expressing as something in my life. I say yes to feelings that promote, encourage, and permit me to express the Image from which I am made. I permit only feelings of joy to flood my being. I am true to my Divine nature. I rejoice in expressing all feelings, images, and thoughts in happiness and glee. Joy and ecstasy radiate from my being. As I speak, the power to restore my feelings, images, and thoughts are in these words. I take delight in my expression. I have all that I need to express my life in joy and love. I am honest and open for channels of good to flow through me freely and generously and lift my mind to express Divine Joy. I am ethical in my assessment of my feelings, images, and thoughts. I am gentle with myself. I reflect genuine strength and happiness. With tolerant understanding, I digest all ideas to increase the flow of Divine Joy in my life. I begin right now, right where I am, making the most of every opportunity that comes my way to express Divine Joy. I fulfill my purpose to express Divine Joy. I am cheerful. I now understand this experience and take responsibility for my thoughts to restore my body, soul, and mind to its original Image. I give thanks as I rise in Joy, filled with Divine Love, to live my life from the Image in which I am made.

Physical State: Body/Dis-ease/Appearance   Diabetes
Emotional State: Soul – bliss, rapture, transport
Mental State: Mind – guilt, sorrow, disappointment
Spiritual State: Law – Joy (undeveloped)

I rise in thought to experience bliss, rapture, and transport – states of the Image in which I am made. It is my Divine Right to express joy in all my activities. I now embrace my feelings, images, and thoughts with joy. I find comfort in knowing I am Divine and I have the freedom to experience Divine Joy in my life. I therefore refute thoughts of guilt, sorrow, and disappointment as I embrace thoughts of innocence, cheer, and acceptance as my way of thinking. I accept, embrace, and court thoughts of Joy. I become still as Divine Joy floods my being. I was created for pleasure and rejoice in my ability to demonstrate happiness and bliss. I find comfort and ease in assessing my feelings, images, and thoughts as opportunities to express Divine Joy. My mind is open and receptive for good to take root, manifest, and demonstrate as perfect health. This event is a re-appointment for me to examine my feelings, images, and thoughts to align with Divine Joy. I am exonerated of all judgments placed on them to participate in activities that bring joy. My faith is strengthened and my expectations are high. I move with certainty through all feelings, images, and thoughts that prevent me from expressing bliss, rapture, and transport. I am at peace. I am encouraged to love myself and to praise this event as good and very good. My assessment of this event is sound. I draw upon the wellspring of wisdom within me to generate new feelings, images, and thoughts. My heart is comforted. I have the incentive to create Divine Joy through this experience. I respond to life in love and allow the Image from which I am made to rise up and fill my life with Divine Joy. I make way for Divine Joy to flood my life. My mind is now clear to express Divine Joy. I am delighted as I realize the purpose of this event and rejoice in this expression. I take in the sweetness of life to heal this condition.

Physical State: Body/Dis-ease/Appearance   Diarrhea
Emotional State: Soul – praise, faith, devotion
Mental State: Mind – dejection, victimhood, escape
Spiritual State: Law – Joy (undeveloped)

I have the intelligence and faith to allow Divine Joy to flow through me to cultivate the Image in which I am made. I have the mental capacity to praise and embrace all feelings, images, and thoughts to express Divine Joy. I reestablish my trust in myself to express Divine Joy. My devotion to the Image in which I am made is strengthened by my loyalty and respect to that Image. I now change my thoughts and declare that I no longer think thoughts of dejection, of victimhood, or escape. I make firm in my mind thoughts that are elated, pure, and free. My feelings, images, and thoughts support my desire to live from that Image, and I embrace thoughts of cheer, approval, and fidelity. Divine Joy floods my life as I regard the Image in which I am made. I honor who I am; I comply with, abide by, and adhere to thoughts that bring Divine Joy. I am attentive, alert, aware, and awake to my feelings, images, and thoughts. I am faithful in my resolve to express Divine Joy. I am at ease. I am at peace. Confidence in my ability to express Divine Joy rises up from within me, and I feel assured that I am capable of expressing Divine Joy through this experience. I move with a certainty and constancy to express Divine Joy. I remember who I am. All feelings, images, and thoughts that are not part of the expression of Divine Joy are now obliterated from my mind. I take the necessary action to change the appearance of feelings, images, and thoughts unlike the Image in which I am made. I am made free by the image in which I am made to govern my life by my thoughts. I take responsibility for all feelings, images, and thoughts right now. I embrace my feelings, images, and thoughts with tenderness and sweetness and comply with them to contribute to the flow of Divine Joy. I have complete confidence in myself to express Divine Joy. In gratitude for the restoration of my thoughts, I express Divine Joy through this experience.

Physical State: Body/Dis-ease/Appearance   Diverticulitis
Emotional State: Soul – unity, concord, rapport, harmony
Mental State: Mind – shy, suspicious, doubtful
Spiritual State: Law – Power (undeveloped)

I remain firm in my conviction to live from the Image in which I am made. I rely upon my inner power and wisdom to guide and direct me into affirmative action. Calm and serene feelings of peace accompany clarity of thought. I am fortified in the knowledge that Good is mine for the asking and awaits my claim. I unify my feelings, images, and thoughts to align for the purpose of expressing Divine Power. I desire to experience rapport and harmony between my feelings, images, and thoughts as I refuse to believe shyness, suspicion, and doubt are necessary to express Divine Power. I accept only thoughts that are bold, friendly, and serene. I allow thoughts of trust and faith to bond my feelings, images, and thoughts. I am uninhibited in my expression to assert my self-worth. I forgive myself as I move forward to accept the Image in which I am made. I am in agreement with myself. I understand who I am and allow this understanding to govern my feelings, images, and thoughts. I am assertive in my efforts to live from that Image. I make friends with my feelings and thoughts. I am gentle with myself in my assessment of my life to restore my health. I am resolved to express Divine Power in all my affairs. I move with assurance upon all decisions made to unleash the essence of the Image in which I am made. My feelings are quiet and at ease. I meet each challenge with confidence and satisfaction. I accomplish my desired good, a good that is right for all concerned. I express the wholeness of life in this experience and accept all events as supportive of my desire to live from the Image in which I am made. I accept and focus on thoughts of unity and peace. I am not alone. My belief is now stabilized to express Divine Power in this experience. I entertain thoughts that are in cooperation and rapport with my true nature. I give thanks that my world is now established in Divine Power.

Physical State: Body/Dis-ease/Appearance   Dry-eye
Emotional State: Soul – Grace, devotion
Mental State: Mind – ugliness, abhorrent, unsightly
Spiritual State: Law – Beauty (undeveloped)

I now look to see the beauty in my feelings, images, and thoughts. I accept the beauty that is inherent within me. I live positively and graciously in thoughts of beauty and love. My life is blessed by the loveliness of the Image in which I am made. I seek only to realize the beauty in my life. The potential of perfection is made visible to me. I no longer indulge in thoughts of ugliness, dislike, and unsightly forms. Instead, I look for and indulge in thoughts of beauty, value, and appeal in all my feelings, images, and thoughts. I value my life and this opportunity to express Divine Beauty. I honor my ability to see through this appearance and see the Beauty in all of my feelings, images, and thoughts. I am devoted to living from that Image. I value, honor, and elevate my thoughts to receive Divine Grace through Divine Power. My awareness of the Image in which I am made increases. As I take pleasure in seeing the beauty in life, my heart becomes that which I behold. My life blossoms forth in exquisite beauty as I respect my feelings, images, and thoughts. I am surrounded by all things, and I call them beautiful. I respect my feelings, images, and thoughts and trust that I have the capacity to express Divine Joy. I affirm, emphatically assert, and embrace only appearances that bring out the Image in which I am made. I call all appearances beautiful, for they are reflections of the Image in which I am made. I am compassionate and generous in uniting my feelings, images, and thoughts, as they are my road map to express Divine Beauty from the Image in which I am made. I handle all experiences with kindness and gentleness. I trust the Image in which I am made to guide me through this experience and to express Divine Joy in everything I do and say. I remember who I am and accept this opportunity to express Divine Beauty in my life, and in my world of affairs. In quiet confidence, I let it go.

Physical State: Body/Affairs   Duty
Emotional State: Soul – obligation, assignment, province
Mental State: Mind – faithless, disloyal, treacherous
Spiritual State: Law – Life (undeveloped)

It is my business to know that I am made in the Image of Perfection and embrace the power to live a Life in peace. I have a responsibility to myself and others. I perform my duty well. I am faithful and honest. My mission is to realize the Image in which I am made. I am conscious of what I feel, what I say, and of what actions I take. I refuse to believe that the experiences of faithlessness, disloyalty, and treachery are necessary for me to experience Divine Life. I state emphatically that I have all the faith that I need to exercise loyalty to my feelings, images, and thoughts. I am true, reliable, and loyal to the Image in which I am made. I depend upon my feelings, images, and thoughts to lead me to and through experiences safely and securely. Life is activity, and I participate in Life. I enjoy Life. I seize this opportunity to bring forth the essence of Life within me. I want to live. I fulfill my duty through Life. I organize my affairs to express more of Life. I discharge my duty with satisfaction. I am filled with vitality. I am substantial. I accept feelings of accountability, allegiance, and fulfillment as I uncover the Image in which I am made. Life is good, and very good. I accept all experiences of Life as part of my duty to uncover the Image in which I am made. I am now free to express Divine Life in Peace and in Harmony. I now realize that anything fabricated from a false sense of life can be destroyed. Every false claim that I have placed on my images, feelings, and thoughts is now null and void. I embrace this experience with joy and gladness.

Physical State: Body/Dis-ease   Ear
Emotional State: Soul – patience, fortitude, endurance
Mental State: Mind – impatience, rejection
Spiritual State: Law – Wisdom (undeveloped)

In this moment, I know that Truth sets me free to express from the Image in which I am made. I claim my gift of wisdom to understand my feelings, images, and thoughts about my life. I open my mind and my ears with enthusiasm to hear the small voice that speaks to me as I accept that Divine Wisdom flows through me. I have the patience, fortitude, and endurance to align my feelings, images, and thoughts to express Divine Wisdom. I am keenly aware of my innate purpose to live from the Image in which I am made and perceive that which is for my highest fulfillment in all situations. I have the capacity to acquire and apply knowledge received from my feelings, images, and thoughts. Therefore, I refuse to believe that thoughts of impatience and rejection are necessary. I affirm and embrace thoughts that are calm, understanding, and accepting to guide me through this experience. I approve, agree, and allow my feelings, images, and thoughts to support me in my resolution to express Divine Power. I am determined to bring forth the qualities of the Image in which I am made and allow them to direct my life. I have the strength and tenacity to heal all images and thoughts and express Divine Power. This experience allows me to become bold and daring in my efforts. I am strong. I invite this event to bring harmony into my feelings, images, and thoughts. I am dauntless. I use good judgment in decision-making, which gives me direction. Everything I do prospers. I have the insight to do what is before me. I choose what I shall think and take action upon my thoughts. Wisdom is my divine gift, and I use my gift wisely in managing my feelings, images, and thoughts. I live in a world of unity. I place my trust in life and am guided in all my undertakings. I accept these words as truth about my life and give thanks for the realization.

Physical State: Body/Affairs   Ecstasy
Emotional State: Soul — awe, exultation, enjoyment
Mental State: Mind — sadness, dejection, despair
Spiritual State: Law — Joy (undeveloped)

I live in a world of wonder and awe. I take delight in knowing the Image in which I am made. I rejoice and give thanks for this experience as I refuse to believe sadness, dejection, and despair are necessary to experience Divine Joy. I accept happy, cheerful, and elated feelings, images, and thoughts in my world. I am lighthearted and have faith in my ability to uncover my Perfection. I am encouraged by this experience to enjoy the wonders of this world. Divine Joy flows through me as I contemplate this event. I revel in the experience and know that Divine Joy fills my very being. I have confidence in myself and look only to the Image in which I am made to understand who I am. I take great pride in this knowing. I am at ease. I am filled with hope. I lift my mind to heights of joy. I am cheerful. I consider this experience as fortunate and flourishing; it brings me to the place in my mind to experience Divine Joy. I am comforted. The essence of prosperity, wealth, and the riches of the Image in which I am made floods my entire Being. I am filled with Light. I am filled with the joy of knowing that I am free to face my feelings, images, and thoughts as part of this experience. I am joyful, cheerful, and filled with glee. As I move through this experience, my being is flooded with the Essence of the Image in which I am made. I am transported to a level of being that radiates Ecstasy. I am in bliss. I am awesome. I realize who I am. I am grateful.

Physical State: Body/Dis-ease/Appearance   Eczema
Emotional State: Soul – enlightenment, fortitude, endurance
Mental State: Mind – offense, irritation, frustration
Spiritual State: Law – Power (undeveloped)

My actions reflect what I feel, what I imagine, and the thoughts that are dominant in my life. I now resolve that my words and my actions motivate me to live from the Image in which I am made. I have the fortitude, endurance, and courage to face any and all situations. I claim my divine right to govern my feelings, images, and thoughts to express Divine Power. I refute thoughts that offend, irritate, or frustrate my feelings and images. I accept only thoughts that please, delight, and satisfy my purpose to live from the Image in which I am made. I embrace and court thoughts that enlighten, appease, and encourage me. I honor, revere, and foster thoughts that enlighten, incite, and motivate me to persevere in this event and heal myself. I forgive myself. I love myself and accept myself just as I am. I am made in the Image of Perfection, having all the necessary essence from that Image to express Divine Power. I have the courage and confidence to move through this experience in peace. I think thoughts that favor and assist me to experience Divine Power. I am now aware, alert, and awake to the Image in which I was made. I see myself as an activity of Life and do those works that I have been given to do. I am an open channel for Divine Power to express through me in every area of my life. The Life that supports me seeks to live through me completely, and I recognize my unity with it. I praise my life. I am the strength of my life. I have all that I need to express Divine Power. I am brave and bold in my assessment of my feelings, images, and thoughts. I tell myself the truth about who I am. I am made in the Image of Perfection, and I accept that power that flows through me to reveal who I am. I live in great expectation of greater experiences to express Divine Power. I am effective. In gratitude and thanksgiving for the revealing of the truth about me, I let it be.

Physical State: Body/Dis-ease/Appearance   Edema
Emotional State: Soul – freedom, activity, empathy
Mental State: Mind – shame, idleness, stagnation
Spiritual State: Law – Power (undeveloped)

I let go of all feelings, images, and thoughts of holding on to that which no longer serves me. I freely let it go and allow for the Image in which I am made to express Divine Power. I am in agreement with myself and all that I do. I am liberated to participate in activities that express Divine Love, authority, order, and government into my life. I accept myself, and I am filled with vim, vigor, and vitality. I am healed. I welcome thoughts of happiness and reject all thoughts of shame, idleness, and stagnation. I accept feelings of self-respect, benefit, and awareness. I court feelings of competence, strength, and might. I have the authority to direct my feelings, images, and thoughts to express Divine Power. I am capable, strong bodied, and sturdy. My feelings, images, and thoughts are guides for me to express Divine Power in this event. I am energetic, robust, and hardy. I am in harmony and agreement with my feelings, images, and thoughts. I approve of myself. I regard the Image in which I am made and now move into favor to express Divine Power. I acknowledge this event as an opportunity to express Divine Power. I welcome all opportunities to free myself from that which is not in harmony with my Image. I am liberated. I am free. I am exonerated. I take action and govern my feelings, images, and thoughts to come into alignment with who I am. The power that is given to me is my divine heritage, and I claim my inheritance now. My life is increased by my right thinking. Divine Order is now established in my thinking, and I walk with certainty and assurance as Divine Power flows through me. I accept, dwell upon, and court thoughts of ease. Relief comes as I become more aware of my true nature. I give thanks for the realization of the truth about this experience.

Physical State: Body/Dis-ease   Elbow
Emotional State: Soul – harmony, duty, mastery
Mental State: Mind – concern, complaining, disorder
Spiritual State: Law – Power (undeveloped)

I integrate my feelings, images, and thoughts to express Divine Power. I am nourished daily from the Image in which I am made, which sustains me in wholeness and guides me into a way of harmonious living that is free. It is my duty to express Divine Power through the Image in which I am made. I now rise to that part of me to express Divine Power. I refute all thoughts of concern, complaining, and disorder as necessary to express Divine Power. I confirm thoughts of affection, praise, and order as the foundation upon which I govern my world. My body is renewed; my mind is refreshed. Every organ, every function, every action and reaction of my body is in harmony with the Image in which I am made, and I consciously unite with it as I know the truth. I have high regard for my feelings, images, and thoughts, and I am flexible in my movement from one thought to another. I am agreeable, open, and caring as I assess my feelings, images, and thoughts to comprehend the purpose of this experience. I am competent, qualified, and have the capacity to take authority over my world of thought and action, and I do so now. I take full responsibility for what I feel, what I imagine, and what I say. I am in appreciation of my life and praise who I am. I take delight in sending out Divine Power through the Image in which I am made. Life is Activity. I affirm my union with Life. I have all the power and vigor necessary for the expression of the Image in which I am made. I accept thoughts of ease and comfort. I am open and receptive to the Divine influx of Power. I accept the circulation of Divine Power, Joy, and Love flowing from the image in which I am made. I exercise tolerance in my understand of this event. I am grateful for this opportunity to express Divine Power, and it is done.

Physical State: Body/Dis-ease   Elimination
Emotional State: Soul – freedom, rapture, devotion
Mental State: Mind – resentment, tension, fear
Spiritual State: Law – Love (undeveloped)

I stand firm upon thoughts filled with Love and Joy. I relax in the realization that I am bathed in Love, in living life, in everlasting Joy. I have a deep sense of Love, enthusiasm, and a passion for life flowing from the Image in which I am made. The qualities of the Image in which I am made fill my entire world with radiant life, with light, and with Love. I have claimed endurance for the Divine flow of Life. I am free to express rapture and devotion through the Image in which I am made, and I am devoted to expressing the very highest qualities of my life. I am free in my expressions of harmony, security, and pleasure in bringing about these qualities. I elevate my assessment of my feelings, images, and thoughts to express Divine Love. Resentment, tension, and fear have no place in my life as I open up to receive only thoughts of approval, relief, and faith to guide me through this experience. I let go all feelings, images, and thoughts that no longer serve me. I forgive myself and appreciate who I am. I allow Divine Love to flood my being. I absolve all images, feelings, and thoughts of yesterday and live in the present moment. I am exonerated from judgments I have placed on my feelings, images, and thoughts. I compliment myself for this experience and move to express Divine Love. I am receptive to the inexhaustible flow of love and the influx of perfect ideas and perfect life. I am free. I embrace Divine Love in everything that I do. I give thanks that the words I now speak in regard to this event are truth, of light, and of love. I accept these words to restore this event to its original purpose. In everything I do, I express Divine Love. I love myself; I praise myself; and I accept myself just as I am.

Physical State: Body/Dis-ease/Appearance   Emphysema
Emotional State: Soul – unity, harmony
Mental State: Mind – unworthiness, conflict, discord
Spiritual State: Law – Life (undeveloped)

I surrender myself to the clear vision and wisdom of the Image in which I am made. Truth removes all confusion. I now accept pure Ideas from that Image and remove self-imposed spiritual blindness. I now draw upon that Image to free myself to become flexible in my assessment of my feelings, images, and thoughts to govern my life. I accept the truth about me. I have the power to succeed. I now establish unity, harmony and accord in my feelings, images, and thoughts to express Divine Life. I am in accord with my life and breath in the breath of Life. I establish solidarity, connectedness, and accord as I evaluate my images, feelings and thoughts about Life. Energy is what I call my feelings and is what I need to dwell in the Image from which I am made. My feelings come to assure me of my aliveness; I nurture my feelings with love and rely upon them to lead me to belief and faith. Therefore, I declare untrue thoughts of unworthiness, conflict and discord as necessary to express Divine Life. I embrace, firmly and emphatically only thoughts that are noble, honorable and exceptional. I dwell upon thoughts of wholeness and alliance that are compatible with the Image in which I am made. I dwell upon thoughts that I can believe about the Image in which I am made. I place great value on my life. I receive the Power to live this life with certainty and conviction as I learn to trust the Image in which I am made. I now feel secure to enjoy life. I remove judgment from my feelings, images, and thoughts and accept that all is good and very good. I depend upon my feelings, images, and thoughts for guidance through this experience to express Divine Life. I bring harmony into my world with my thoughts and I change my thinking to express Divine Life. My thoughts are important. I am grateful for this realization of the truth about my life and world of affairs. I express Divine Life in Love.

Physical State: Body/Dis-ease/Appearance   Energy (lack of)
Emotional State: Soul – serenity, tranquility, repose
Mental State: Mind – sadness, grief, anxiety
Spiritual State: Law – Peace (undeveloped)

I give complete recognition of the ability of the Image in which I am made. My mind is open that I may learn the truth about the Image in which I am made. I expect a greater truth to be revealed to me every day. I expect to learn how to relax and be at peace. I am concerned with the present moment and keep my feelings, images, and thoughts in the moment. I consciously raise my thoughts to unite with that Image from which I am made and I am at peace. I am tranquil and serene. I rest in sweet repose. I am confident, content and at ease with my feelings, images, and thoughts. I now abstain from thoughts of sadness, grief and anxiety as I declare that only thoughts of happiness, consolation, and assurance are now pervading my world of thought. I am bold in spirit, reassured of my security and self-confidence as I trust the Image in which I am made. I rise in quiet contemplation to express Divine Peace. I find equanimity in my evaluation of my life to bring glee, cheerfulness and calmness to my world. I am content. Harmony fills my being. I no longer resist my feelings, images, and thoughts and cooperate with life. I start now with gratitude for the fulfillment of my life. I now understand the purpose of this experience and welcome the opportunity to live from the Image in which I am made. I am filled with vim, vigor and vitality. My spirit soars. I am encouraged to move through this experience knowing that I am not separated from life. I am in agreement with all thoughts as they are support for the unfolding of the Image in which I am made. I rest in the light of my soul. I bless the presence of all feelings, images, and thoughts. I am subjected only to recognizing Divine Peace that flow through my feelings, images, and thoughts. Divine Peace is the source of my inspiration, illumination, and revelation for the Image in which I am made. In joy, peace, and thanksgiving, it is done.

Physical State: Body/Affairs   Envy
Emotional State: Soul – ability, insight, depth
Mental State: Mind – resentment, spite
Spiritual State: Law – Wisdom (undeveloped)

I approve of myself and all my possessions. I am grateful for all that I have. I welcome every opportunity to praise who I am and give thanks. I have the ability to draw to me that which is rightfully mine and reach within me to think clearly and precisely. I refuse to believe that thoughts of resentment and spite are necessary. I accept only thoughts of pleasure, goodwill, and kindness. I assess my feelings, images, and thoughts to move through any and all events. I congratulate myself on all my accomplishments and know that everything I need is already provided for me. I am considerate of myself. I have the foresight to move through my feelings, images, and thoughts. I have the perception to discern that which is true and that which is false. I accept feelings of contentment and forgiveness as needed in all expressions of Divine Wisdom. I am at ease in allowing Divine Love and Divine Wisdom to flow through me to uncover the Image in which I am made. I am humble in my approach to life. My perception of good is based upon my desire to unfold my greatest potential. I have all that I require to accomplish my heart's desire. I praise that which I am. I become patient in my understanding of who I am. I look to myself for completion. I regard each idea in high esteem as my vision of my Divine nature unfolds. I turn from every undesirable appearance. I clear my mind of any and all sense of separation from who I am. I have increased knowing of my Indwelling Perfection. I praise the Image in which I am made. For this I am grateful.

Physical State: Body/Dis-ease   Eye
Emotional State: Soul – unity, truth, grace
Mental State: Mind – bitterness, remorse, hostility
Spiritual State: Law – Beauty (undeveloped)

I am made in the Image of Perfection, and I see through the eyes of that Image. My life is full and balanced because I am continuously aware of the Image in which I am made. I unite in truth to allow Grace to flow from the Image in which I am made into my world to express Divine Beauty. I free myself from the limited belief that any mistake for which I have been judged has power to limit my life. My feelings, images, and thoughts come to stabilize, benefit, and support my receptivity to the experience of Divine Beauty. I declare thoughts of bitterness, remorse, and hostility to be untrue. I declare, maintain, and confirm only thoughts that are gentle, satisfying, and agreeable. I take care and good stewardship in assessing all feelings, images, and thoughts that govern my being. I draw upon my value, splendor, and magnificence to radiate excellence from the Image in which I am made. Divine Beauty is my inheritance. I forgive myself, appreciate myself, and I am thankful for who I am. I express Divine Beauty, which is my nature. I am amply supplied with love for the development of my Divine Beauty. I am enthusiastic in my desire to express the wholeness of my being. I draw upon my storehouse of vitality; Love attends me here. I remain true, upright, and honest in expressing my feelings, images, and thoughts as the essence of Divine Beauty in this experience. I remain at peace. I pursue and dwell upon thoughts that express Divine Beauty. I take responsibility for bringing Divine Beauty into my life, and I live from the Image in which I am made. The truth is now established as my true nature. In gratitude, I express good stewardship to allow Divine Beauty to flow freely and unobstructed through my body.

Physical State: Body/Dis-ease   Face
Emotional State: Soul – discernment, trust, duty
Mental State: Mind – judgment, rejection, anxiety
Spiritual State: Law – Power (undeveloped)

I am gentle in my assessment of my feelings, images, and thoughts. With keen awareness, I perceive that this experience is for the purpose of allowing me to realize the Image in which I am made. I trust this event to lead me to that Image. I remain firm in my conviction of the truth of who I am and rely upon my inner power and wisdom to lead, guide, and direct me into affirmative action. It is my duty to express the Image in which I am made. I meet each challenge with confidence and satisfaction. I accomplish my desired good, a good that is right for all concerned. I refuse to accept judgment, rejection, and anxiety as necessary. I accept thoughts that allow me to move through this experience with brave decisions, acceptable solutions, and calm feelings. I remain valiant, courageous, and brave as I am reassured by the Image in which I am made. I am calm, peaceful, and relieved. I think thoughts that are substantial and durable, with a certainty that this event is for my highest good. I love, cherish, and favor my feelings, images, and thoughts. I forgive myself. I am resolved to express Divine Power in all my affairs. My affairs are now established in peace. I am in accord with my feelings, images, and thoughts. I recognize and claim Divine Power right now. I am composed and tranquil as thoughts of wholeness pervade my mind. I accept this event as supportive of my experience to live from the Image in which I am made. I live consistently in the midst of good as Divine Power flows through me. I am showered with blessings and receive them graciously and gratefully. My trust is now reestablished in the Image in which I am made. I am dauntless in my resolve to live from that Image in this experience. I give thanks for the graciousness of life, for life is good and very good. I accept this event as good.

Physical State: Body/Affairs/Appearance   Faith (lack of)
Emotional State: Soul – trust, reliance, fidelity
Mental State: Mind – doubt, mistrust, denial
Spiritual State: Law – Power (undeveloped)

My faith sustains my expectancy at all times. As is my faith, so is my acceptance of my feelings, images, and thoughts. My faith in Life depends upon my acceptance and my expectancy of Divine Power. I place confidence in myself. I refuse to believe that thoughts of doubt, mistrust, and denial are necessary. I accept only trust, reliance, and fidelity as a foundation on which to build my faith. I am devoted to bringing forth the Image in which I am made. I rejoice in receiving wisdom and understanding as I grow in Faith. Everything I do prospers as I fully accept the power that is within the Image in which I am made. I am honest with myself. I pledge loyalty and allegiance to bring forth the power that is within my feelings, images, and thoughts. I dwell upon those thoughts that bring me in harmony with my whole being. I face Life squarely. I call upon the vitality, vim, and vigor of that Image to move through this experience in peace and in harmony. I move with confidence to a place where I am free to express Divine Power. My faith is in my ability to assess my feelings, images, and thoughts to experience Divine Power. I am strong, capable, and I take responsibility for that Image. I expect only good. I move into the wellspring deep within me to receive Divine Power and express in the Image in which I am made. I believe in the truth about me. I am certain of and give credence to the Truth. I am vividly aware of my true nature, as I know my life has purpose. I move in confidence and assurance that this is the truth.

Physical State: Body/Dis-ease/Appearance Fat
Emotional State: Soul – prosperity, providence, duty
Mental State: Mind – insecurity, resistance, anger
Spiritual State: Law – Joy (undeveloped)

I see the good in perfecting the Image in which I am made. Within me is that which is perfect and complete. It is that which is my life, truth, and action. I am assured of an eternal response to my faith in and acceptance of the Image. I understand the meaning of living from the Image in which I am made. I am prosperous and have the capacity to live from the Image in which I am made. I draw upon the wealth of that which I am to express Divine Joy. It is my duty to express the qualities of my Image, and I am certain that I have every advantage and opportunity to do so. I am loved, and as I submit to this event, I am calm and delighted with my progress. I refuse to believe that insecurity, resistance, and anger are necessary. Divine Joy flows through me to express abundant life. I affirm and embrace thoughts that are free to experience Divine Joy. I comply with my feelings, images, and thoughts as I become patient with myself. I love myself. Divine Joy is my inheritance, and I am blessed. I am productive in all my undertakings and move with gladness of heart to express Divine Joy. I accept this experience as a guide to my greater understanding of the Image in which I am made. I am constantly aware of feelings, images, and thoughts to create an abundant life. I am fortunate. I feel a sense of joy as I turn to the Image in which I am made. My only responsibility in life is to respond to the Image in which I am made. I move through life with fervor and zeal. Divine Joy is my innate nature, and I rise to my true nature now to express the Image in which I am made. I am in cooperation with life. I am obedient to Life. My thoughts are centered upon expectancy and Joy. I reestablish my world to recognize the Divine Joy that is within me. In quiet peace, gratitude, and Joy, I give thanks that the purpose of this experience is revealed to me.

Physical State: Body/Dis-ease/Appearance   Fatigue
Emotional State: Soul – mercy, rapture, enthusiasm
Mental State: Mind – angry, lazy, apathetic
Spiritual State: Law - Life (undeveloped)

I praise the life I am. I am conscious of an Infinite Love, renewed faith, and complete security. I align myself with the powers of goodness and right action. I abide in perfect and complete peace as I recognize the Image in which I am made. I am grateful for this experience as I move with eagerness to live from the Image in which I am made. I am revitalized, replenished, and invigorated as I accept this opportunity to express Divine Life. I am filled with vim, vivacity, and vigor as I move with boldness and with fervor into the Image in which I am made. I am filled with ecstasy. My heart is filled with gratitude. I am diligent in reviewing my feelings, images, and thoughts to express Divine Life. I move through any and all events in peace. I refute thoughts of anger, laziness, and apathy. I support thoughts of love, activity, and passion as the foundation upon which I stand to express Divine Life. I am compassionate, kind, and forgiving of my feelings, images, and thoughts in order to express Divine Life from the Image in which I am made. I acknowledge my innate ability to express life and seek those activities that bring courage. I am filled with anticipation as I understand Divine Life as the essence of the Image in which I am made. I turn to my feelings, images, and thoughts to guide me and to support me in this experience. I am filled with zeal. I am thrilled. I am patient in my understanding of my feelings, images, and thoughts as I enthusiastically discover the Image in which I am made. I praise my life. My mind is now filled with loving, kind, and gentle thoughts. I now invite and accept with full cooperation inspiration, illumination, and guidance from the Image in which I am made. I give thanks for the opportunity to know the truth about this event; and in absolute faith, perfect peace, and unbinding joy, I continue to praise the Image in which I am made.

Physical State: Body/Affairs   Fear
Emotional State: Soul – endurance, confidence, faith
Mental State: Mind – suspicion, terror, dread
Spiritual State: Law – Power (undeveloped)

I keep my mind open and receptive to new Ideas. I feel calm and secure in my assessment of my feelings, images, and thoughts. I include every part of my life in my activities. I remove the judgment from my feelings, images, and thoughts. I am safe and calm. I am confident that I can move through this experience to strengthen the Image in which I am made. All experiences are to guide me to that Image. I draw upon Divine Power. My faith is restored. I have the endurance to move joyfully and peacefully through this and all experiences to radiate Divine Power. I refute feelings of fear and thoughts of mistrust, terror and dread as necessary to express Divine Power. I approve of thoughts and feelings of endurance, confidence, and assurance that I am made in the Image of Perfection. I rise now to that Image. I strengthen my faith in my ability to express Divine Power. I have dominion over my feelings and thoughts. I command of myself to take leadership and move through this experience. I am free to express Divine Power through this experience. I am strong. My confidence radiates understanding, power, and strength. I am tranquil and at peace. I have faith and draw upon faith to sustain me in this moment. I rely upon the assurance that Divine Power supports me in this and all events. I let go of fear this moment and take a firm grip on my feelings, images, and thoughts. I embrace thoughts of truth. I trust completely and fully in my feelings, images, and thoughts to guide me to the Image in which I am made. I clarify my thinking and feelings to see the good. I am bold and filled with valor as I move confidently through this experience, giving thanks.

Physical State: Body/Dis-ease/Appearance   Female Problems
Emotional State: Soul – trust, confidence, endurance
Mental State: Mind – fear, guilt, inadequacy
Spiritual State: Law – Love (undeveloped)

I turn from undesirable appearances and clear my mind of any and all separation from the Image in which I am made. I look to myself for completion. I regard each feeling, image and thought in high esteem as my vision of my divine nature makes awareness of Its Presence. I am patient in my understanding of me. I have the capacity to express Divine Love in this and all events in my world. I have an increased awareness of who I am. Love embraces all and I am free to accept only love, forgiveness and joy. I trust the Image in which I am made and have confidence that I have the endurance to express Divine Love. I love myself. Love embraces all of my feelings, images, and thoughts. I am created out of love and love is the very essence of me. I revere the Life of me, worshiping the very essence of me. I am true to myself. I trust myself. I embrace thoughts that promote, encourage, and permit the flow of Divine Love. Therefore, I declare thoughts of fear, guilt, and inadequacy to be untrue. I declare thoughts of bravery, innocence, and sufficiency to be true. I stand firm upon my approval and acceptance of every feeling, image, and thought. I seize life with passion and fervor. I am immersed in truth in a perfect life. I am courageous. I hold to feelings, images, and thoughts of assurance, honor, and certitude. I have faith and expand my faith to the Image in which I am made. I love and approve of myself just as I am. I praise myself for who I am. I am free to express Divine Love through my thought. I accept and embrace only feelings, images, and thoughts of contentment and forgiveness of my feelings, images, and thoughts. My feelings are compatible with my purpose to express Divine Love. I am bold and valiant. Divine Love heals my body, soul, and mind. I now recognize the truth about myself. I am now free to experience the totality of life and express Divine Love through the Image in which I am made.

Physical State: Body/Dis-ease/Appearance　Fever
Emotional State: Soul — order, forthrightness, justice
Mental State: Mind — anger, resistance, stubbornness
Spiritual State: Law — Love (undeveloped)

I turn my attention to acceptance of and obedience to the Image in which I am made. In my thought is the power; in my heart is the radiance; and in my body is the substance of the Image in which I am made. My thought is brought to order as I exemplify forthrightness and justice in assessing my feelings, images, and thoughts. I accept all appearances as guidance for me to unfold the Image in which I am made. It is imperative that I face the truth of myself and bring goodness and mercy into my feelings, images, and thoughts. I refuse to accept thoughts of anger, resistance, and stubbornness as necessary to express Divine Love. I accept, affirm, and embrace feelings of forgiveness, liberation, and surrender to this event to express from the Image in which I am made. I hold dear and am devoted to caring for the Image in which I am made. I am agreeable, flexible, and open to receiving Divine Love in this event. I welcome the opportunity to receive Divine Love. I am open, straightforward, and honest in my evaluation of my feelings, images, and thoughts. I expand my thought to include kindness, receptivity, and devotion to the Image in which I am made. I am liberated as I surrender all judgment placed on my actions, and I welcome the change. I praise myself for the change. I am willing to change. I embrace thoughts that are supportive of the change to express Divine Love. I become calm and centered as Divine Love flows through me. I trust my feelings, images, and thoughts to guide me to the Image in which I am made. I tell myself the truth about me. All feelings, images, and thoughts promote, facilitate, and expedite the essence of Divine Love as it flows through me. I am loved. I am relieved as I realize the Image in which I am made. I gain the strength to reconcile all feelings, images, and thoughts in harmony with the Image in which I am made. In gratitude and thanksgiving for this realization, I let it be.

Physical State: Body/Dis-ease/Appearance   Fibromyalgia
Emotional State: Soul — unity, harmony, trust
Mental State: Mind — despair, distrust, dread
Spiritual State: Law — Joy (undeveloped)

The Image in which I am made directs all organs of my body so that each functions perfectly according to its true nature. Divine Joy is at the center of my being, and I call it forth now to express through me to restore my body to wholeness and harmony. I have complete confidence, trust, and faith in the Image in which I am made for this restoration. The power is within the words that I speak. The calm, continuous pulsations of Life are governed by Divine Joy. I decline and abstain from indulging in thoughts of despair, distrust, and dread. I accept and indulge in thoughts that are courageous, trusting, and hopeful. I feel secure. I have a zest for life and enhance my self-worth with activities that bring Divine Joy. I rejoice in expressing all thoughts in happiness and awe. I am free to face Life from the Image in which I am made. Joy and ecstasy radiate from the Image in which I am made. I am spontaneous and, therefore, I am free to express happiness and pleasure in all my experiences. I am filled with Divine Joy. I now live my life in joy and harmony. The Image in which I am made is my life, and I represent that Life in my expressions of cheerfulness, gladness, and security. Love fills my life. Divine Joy fills my being. I am at peace with who and what I am. I love and accept myself as the Image in which I am made and take delight in this expression. I bring joyous activity into my life. I have all that I need to express Divine Joy and Divine Love. I trust who I am. I am unified in feelings, images, and thoughts to express the true nature of the Image in which I am made. I am open and honest with myself and embrace my feelings, images, and thoughts in this event to express Divine Joy. I am at peace. I am now free to express Divine Joy in all my activities, and I seize every opportunity to make this expression in love. I now claim Divine Love as the power that governs my feelings, images, and thoughts. I give thanks.

Physical State: Body/Dis-ease   Foot
Emotional State: Soul – discernment, conviction, fervor
Mental State: Mind – fear, confusion
Spiritual State: Law – Wisdom (undeveloped)

I now turn to my feelings, images, and thoughts to determine what is right and best for me in this event. I start this day by first forgiving myself for past mistakes or wrong judgments. I give for love, and I harbor kind thoughts and dwell on kind deeds. I now elevate myself by accepting my feelings, images, and thoughts as part of the Image in which I am made to express Divine Wisdom. Order pervades my mind. I am motivated by patience and understanding. I am gentle as I discern my conviction to express Divine Wisdom with fervor though my feelings, images, and thoughts. I refuse to admit thoughts of fear and confusion into my mind as I accept only thoughts of courage, clarity, and good judgment to enter and take root. I perceive this experience to express Divine Wisdom. I am in awe as I assess my feelings, images, and thoughts for a greater understanding of the Image in which I am made. I trust who I am and claim my capacity to express Divine Wisdom in this event. I am capable and intelligent, and I comprehend my purpose in life. I draw upon the wellspring of knowledge to move into the Image in which I am made. I view all experiences as favorable, trustworthy, and evident of the Image in which I am made. I change my attitude to one of kindness, friendliness, and benevolence in discerning my feelings, images, and thoughts. I am patient and submissive to the influx of Divine Wisdom that flows through me in all events. My belief is firmly rooted in truth, as I am certain that all feelings, images, and thoughts rise out of the Image in which I am made. I am humble in my approach as I discern the purpose of this event. I have all that I need to accomplish my desire to express Divine Wisdom in my life. I regard each event as an opportunity to express Divine Wisdom. I am now free to experience Divine Wisdom, reestablishing my conviction of the Image in which I am made. In thanksgiving and praise for who I am, I am at peace.

Physical State: Body/Affairs   Forgiveness
Emotional State: Soul – absolution, exoneration, release
Mental State: Mind – rejection, guilt, anxiety
Spiritual State: Law – Love/Peace (undeveloped)

I forgive myself and everyone, and everyone forgives me. Forgiving and being forgiven, I now have an inward sense of peace and tranquility. I understand my union with all life, and I know there is no judgment against me from my feelings, images, and thoughts. I desire to give love, express kindness, and exhibit strength, peace, and beauty from the Image in which I am made. I am absolved, exonerated, and released to express Divine Love and Divine Peace through my feelings, images, and thoughts. I refuse to believe thoughts of rejection, guilt, and anxiety as necessary to experience Divine Love and Divine Peace. I embrace, affirm, and court thoughts of acceptance, innocence, and relief to express Divine Love and Divine Peace. I am free. My feelings, images, and thoughts reflect my need to forgive myself and others. All others are mirrors of me to remind me to love and forgive myself. I acknowledge all appearances of the need to give love. Appearances come to guide me to my true nature and to teach me to live within the Image in which I am made. I harbor no unkind thoughts. I dwell upon thoughts of kindness. I give myself love for past mistakes or wrong judgments. My life and experiences have greater meaning for me. I seek to express the splendor and majesty of the Image in which I am made. I can now move with confidence and certainty to express that Image. I am free to Love. I open my heart and my mind to accept the Divine Love and Divine Peace that are mine by Divine Right. I am filled with the joy of love that comes when I forgive myself and all others. I now move to live from the Image in which I am made.

Physical State: Body/Dis-ease/Appearance   Frigidity
Emotional State: Soul – exaltation, ecstasy, duty
Mental State: Mind – resentment, guilt, bitterness
Spiritual State: Law – Joy (undeveloped)

I approach my feelings, images, and thoughts in a loving, passionate, and amiable manner. I am loyal, trustworthy, and dutiful in unfolding and expressing Divine Joy. My agreement is with myself to live from the Image in which I am made. I am unlimited in my expression of this Image. I exalt my thoughts to experience ecstasy from the Image in which I am made. I refuse to dwell upon thoughts of resentment, guilt, and bitterness. I dwell upon, court, and approve of thoughts of praise, merriment, and lightheartedness. I am appreciative, friendly, and amiable for the knowledge of the Image in which I am made. I strengthen my faith through this experience. I am warm and loving. I move through all fears to embrace the Image in which I am made, and I am exalted by this action to express Divine Joy. I draw from my Image all that I need to express Divine Joy. Love heals all wounds, and I grasp this healing balm right now. I am dutiful in recognizing all feelings, images, and thoughts as my appointment for greater experiences. I abide in and remain steadfast in my desire to express Divine Joy. I accept my freedom to reveal the Image in which I am made. I rededicate my life to my conviction for expressing Divine Joy. I am loyal, trustworthy, and reliable in discerning all feelings, images, and thoughts to aid my resolve to live from the Image in which I am made. I accept only thoughts that aid, support, and purport my desire to live from the Image in which I am made. All feelings, images, and thoughts are desirable, serviceable, and superior to any judgment I have placed upon them. I am obedient, worthy, and successful in governing my thoughts to receive innovative Ideas to express Divine Joy. I am open to receive. I love and praise myself just as I am. I feel secure as I give thanks for this event that leads me to the Image in which I am made.

Physical State: Body/Dis-ease/Appearance   Fungus
Emotional State: Soul – deftness, mastery
Mental State: Mind – disagreeable, inadequate
Spiritual State: Law – Power (undeveloped)

All desires are good, as desire comes from the Image in which I am made for me to create a life of love, joy, and happiness. I seek to fulfill my agreement with my feelings, images, and thoughts to express Divine Power. My mind is quickened to action as I realize the purpose of this experience to express Divine Power. I open up to receive from the bounteous storehouse of the Image in which I am made and express Divine Power through this experience. Divine Love flows through me as the fragrance from a flower. I am proficient in my efforts to express Divine Power. I have dominion over my feelings, images, and thoughts, and I take command right now as I deny thoughts of disagreement and inadequacy. I affirm, embrace, and harbor only thoughts that are skillful, agile, and authoritative. Confidence and strength guide me though this event to express from the Image in which I am made. I am dauntless in my pursuit. I am devoted to the Image in which I am made, and I express Divine Power through this experience. I accept, select, and dwell upon thoughts of success, aid, and support. I am filled with vigor and vitality; I am capable of moving forward in my desire to express Divine Power. I let go of all that is not accepting of who I am. The quality of my feelings, images, and thoughts is sound, superior, and active as my guidepost to lead me to the Image in which I am made. I honor myself. I love myself. I praise myself. I love and honor the Image in which I am made. Divine Power flowing through me brings relief and quickens a new interest for life. I cooperate with and actively participate in all feelings, images, and thoughts to bring about my union with the Image in which I am made. I make peace with myself. My mind is open to receive the desires of my heart, and I am fulfilled. I accept this knowing in peace and thanksgiving, allowing Divine Power to flow through me.

Physical State: Body/Dis-ease　Gall Bladder
Emotional State: Soul – gratitude, purpose, duty
Mental State: Mind – anger, bitterness
Spiritual State: Law – Joy (undeveloped)

I enter into the joy of conscious union with the Image in which I am made. I align myself with the powers of goodness and right action. I abide in complete faith in the Image in which I am made. I am filled with gratitude as my purpose is revealed to me to embrace my duty to live from the Image in which I am made. I refuse to believe thoughts of anger and bitterness as necessary to express Divine Joy. I make firm in my mind only loving thoughts that inspire me to live from the Image in which I am made. I now view my feelings, images, and thoughts in a different light. I express Divine Joy in unselfish ways. I find comfort in having my purpose and the freedom to experience Divine Joy. I embrace life with fondness, as I have the assurance of the Image in which I am made. I am daring, bold, and brave as I assess my feelings, images, and thoughts. I am valiant, reliable, and grateful for the experience to live from the Image in which I am made. I have mastery over my feelings, images, and thoughts and face my obligation to respond in love to express Divine Joy. I am attentive to my desire to express from the Image in which I am made. I feel secure and tranquil in my ability to develop the Image in which I am made. Order pervades my mind. I live in a constant state of Peace. I give love to my feelings, images, and thoughts as I praise who I am. I love myself. I start this day by forgiving myself for past mistakes and misjudgments. I now elevate my thoughts by accepting my feelings, images, and thoughts as my guides for living from the Image in which I am made. I humbly receive all thoughts as they are presented to me, and I see the good in each one. I am patient in my understanding of myself as I enthusiastically discover the Image in which I am made. I give thanks for the opportunity for this experience that draws me into the Image in which I am made.

Physical State: Body/Dis-ease/Appearance   Gallstones
Emotional State: Soul – honor, humility, meekness
Mental State: Mind – condemnation, resistance
Spiritual State: Law – Peace (undeveloped)

I dare to face life, to see through the appearance until I recognize the perfection and Wholeness of Good in my feelings, images, and thoughts. I become aware of that deep, abiding peace that quiets and stills every thought, steadies every nerve, and forever balances life's circulation of Divine Peace through my body. I submit to the Image in which I am made as I resign myself to expressing Divine Peace through this experience. I honor the Image in which I am made. I exalt my feelings, images, and thoughts to have faith in the Integrity of the Image in which I am made. I am modest in my assessment of my thoughts. I now deny thoughts of condemnation and resistance as a way for me to express Divine Peace. I affirm, court, and maintain thoughts of praise, truth, and humility as the foundation for my thoughts. I sort through my feelings, images, and thoughts and separate them to regain equanimity. Divine Peace lulls, soothes, and comforts me. I turn in thought to the Image in which I am made and unify with who I am. I accept an abundance of Joy in its totality as necessary for my resolve to live from the Image in which I am made. I am undisturbed by adverse appearances as I surrender to the Image in which I am made. I now recognize that each endeavor is intended to express Divine Peace with enthusiasm and understanding. This unity of interest, enthusiasm, and understanding develops Divine Peace for me to live from the Image in which I am made. I accept this experience as a privilege for me to embrace my feelings, images, and thoughts to live from the Image in which I am made. I place my full vision, faith, and love in the Image in which I am made. I am encouraged by feelings of empathy, union, and agreement to express Divine Peace. I embrace feelings that produce peace. I am at ease. I am calm. I am at peace. In quiet confidence and thanksgiving for the revelation of the truth about me, I accept that it is done.

Physical State: Body/Affairs/Dis-ease   Generosity
Emotional State: Soul – unselfishness, nobility
Mental State: Mind – stingy, miserly, selfish
Spiritual State: Law – Joy/Power (undeveloped)

I turn to the Giver of Life and reaffirm my unity with all of Life. I now bless my feelings, images, and thoughts. I have faith that my word cannot return to me void. I now embrace the Image in which I am made to enhance my life and all who come into my world. I am free to experience the bountifulness of this world. I stand open-handed, ready to receive so that I may share. I am kind and gentle with myself. I refuse thoughts of stinginess, miserliness, and selfishness as necessary to experience Divine Joy and Divine Power. I know my purpose. I take great joy in fulfilling my purpose. I am in agreement with my feelings, images, and thoughts to experience Divine Joy and Divine Power. I accept the good that I have and praise the good that I receive. I am opulent and munificent. I am gentle, caring, and loving. I am considerate in examining my feelings, images, and thoughts to bring forth Divine Joy and Divine Power. As I open up to give, I receive the very essence of Divine Joy and Divine Power. I acknowledge my Divine potential for living, and I nourish and encourage it. I fully accept the power that is within me. I now choose to stand firm upon my decision to be generous. I am liberal, charitable, and considerate of my feelings, images, and thoughts. I am tolerant of who I am. I practice good will and give love to my feelings, images, and thoughts. I accept Divine Joy and Divine Power in this moment. Divine Power is my heritage, and I claim it now. Patience with myself allows me to accept all feelings, images, and thoughts about all events. I draw upon my inner strength to do that which I need to do. I am grateful and giving.

Physical State: Body/Dis-ease/Appearance   Goiter
Emotional State: Soul — harmony, mastery
Mental State: Mind — victimhood, helplessness, anger
Spiritual State: Law — Power (undeveloped)

I keep my mind open and receptive to new ideas. I include every part of my life in all my activity. I respect my feelings, images, and thoughts, and now remove all judgments that I have placed upon them. I realize that fear subtracts from my confidence. I embrace courage as I face the facts and call upon the Image in which I am made. I have regard for my feelings, images, and thoughts. I hold steadfastly, undaunted, and consistent in my desire to express Divine Power through this experience. I am supported by the Image in which I am made. I call upon harmony to assist me in bringing mastery to my feelings, images, and thoughts. Therefore, I refuse to accept the appearance of being a helpless, angry victim. I accept thoughts of innocence, power, and love to support the Image in which I am made. I cling to thoughts of agreement, accord, and unity to restore Divine Power in my life. I have the capacity, strength, and ability to live from the Image in which I am made. The quality of my thought strengthens my world to express Divine Power. I am filled with vigor and vitality. I am consistent in my desire to express Divine Power. My feelings, images, and thoughts are my guideposts to live from the Image in which I am made. I allow Divine Wisdom to guide me into the path of right conduct in my life. I clarify my feelings, images, and thoughts to accept assurance, confidence, and vigor as true discernment of my desire to live from the Image in which I am made. I rely upon the assurance that Divine Power supports me in this and all experiences. I draw upon my faith to restore the truth of my purpose to express Divine Power. I am tranquil and at peace. I rest in quietude and sweet repose. My confidence radiates understanding, power, and strength. I call this experience good and very good as I now realize the purpose. I am grateful for this realization.

Physical State: Body/Dis-ease/Appearance   Gout
Emotional State: Soul — discernment, acceptance
Mental State: Mind — impatience, anger, revenge
Spiritual State: Law — Wisdom (undeveloped)

I begin this moment to forgive myself for past mistakes and unsound judgments. I let go all unkind thoughts. I now perceive the purpose of this experience and move into accepting the purpose as Divine. I express patience in my understanding of the Image in which I am made. I embrace my feelings, images, and thoughts as my perception of this event is made clear. I have keen sight. I am agreeable and forgiving to ascertain and express Divine Wisdom. I allow the essence of Divine Wisdom to flow though me to guide me to the Image in which I am made. As I center my attention on who I am, I meet all situations in my life with poise and assurance. I am wise in my assessment of my feelings, images, and thoughts. I am intelligent and call upon that Intelligence from the Image in which I am made. I am pleased. I refuse to accept thoughts of impatience, anger, and revenge. Appearances are not real, and I can change all appearances as I change my feelings, images, and thoughts. I do so now. I accept only thoughts that are serene and loving, and I am pardoned. I acknowledge the Image in which I am made and seize every opportunity to learn Divine Wisdom through every experience. I no longer worship anything outside of me, as only that which I am is fulfilling. The very essence of the Image in which I am made is within me, and I surrender all feelings, images, and thoughts into its keeping. I remove all barriers and allow Divine Wisdom to fill my thoughts with the substance of faith. I accept and embrace thoughts of truth, agreement, and praise. This acceptance governs the course of my realization of the Image in which I am made. I hold firmly to thoughts that are cheerful, wise, and calming. My vision is clear as I accept all feelings, images, and thoughts as necessary to realize the Image in which I am made. Guidance comes with wisdom. I am relieved. I am at peace. I give thanks for the revealing of truth right now.

Physical State: Body/Affairs   Greed
Emotional State: Soul – generous, benevolent, full
Mental State: Mind – selfishness, stinginess, voracity
Spiritual State: Law - Power (undeveloped)

Right where I am, I am established in richness and the abundance of Good. Success and prosperity meet me from every side. I open my mind to receive Divine Ideas of Power. I give generously. It is my joy to give richly, and I am aware of being a gracious receiver. Generosity is my true nature, as I am made in the Image of Perfection, and my true nature is to give. As I give, I must receive. I refuse to believe that selfishness, stinginess, and voracity are needed in my life to express Divine Power. I have sovereignty over my feelings, images, and thoughts. I am satiated. I accept only thoughts of selflessness, lavishness, and generosity as I experience Divine Power. I am considerate as I assess my feelings, images, and thoughts of any and all events in my life. I consider all feelings, images, and thoughts as guides to lead me to uncover that Perfection. I am enough; I have enough. I am liberal in my thinking. I am satisfied with who I am. There can only be a re-giving of all that I have to my feelings, images, and thoughts. I give generously, unstintingly, and freely. I have enough to spare and to share. There is no lack of abundance in life, and I cannot know lack in my life. I change the appearance now to heal this attitude. I recognize all feelings, images, and thoughts as my signals to develop the Image in which I am made. All that I receive is from the Image in which I am made. The endless, boundless Life from within the Image in which I am made fills my entire being. I accept all desires as one—to express only good. I recognize the abundance of Good and praise the Life that I am. I am thankful for this realization.

Physical State: Body/Dis-ease   Gums
Emotional State: Soul – judiciousness, gratitude, meekness
Mental State: Mind – procrastination, haste
Spiritual State: Law – Wisdom (undeveloped)

I now center my attention on who I am. I meet all situations in my life with poise and assurance. I strive for understanding and endeavor to use this knowledge in my relationship with myself as all barriers fall away. I now allow Divine Wisdom to fill my thoughts with substance and faith. I am wise, appreciative, and meek in assessing my feelings, images, and thoughts about my life. I trust the Image in which I am made to lead me to the fulfillment of my desire to express Divine Wisdom. I refuse to accept thoughts of procrastination and haste as I accept only thoughts that are expeditious and quicken me to receive Divine Power. I am aided in every experience by the Image in which I am made. I understand and accept all thoughts as necessary to comprehend, acknowledge, and appreciate the Image in which I am made. My judgments are sound, intelligent, and wise in my assessment of my feelings, images, and thoughts. I am thoughtful, prudent, and teachable in my recognition of the Image in which I am made. I am practical and humble in my approach to all events. I embrace thoughts with joy. My thoughts come to serve me, and I direct all thoughts to prosper in my desire to live from the Image in which I am made. I move boldly and confidently through life, trusting the Image in which I am made to guide me to the one supreme idea to express Divine Wisdom. Wisdom flows with love. Guidance comes with wisdom. I surrender my human sense of self and draw upon the Divine. I know the truth, and the truth sets me free. I stand firm in my conviction to live from the Image in which I am made. I have a sense of certainty and security because I trust who I am. I give thanks for my freedom to live from the Image of who I am.

Physical State: Body/Affairs   Hate
Emotional State: Soul – love, regard, devotion
Mental State: Mind – dislike, abhorrence, enmity
Spiritual State: Law – Love (undeveloped)

Love is the healer of my feelings, images, and thoughts to develop the Image in which I am made. I cherish my feelings, images, and thoughts, as they are my road map to a joy-filled and loving atmosphere. I treasure the feelings of love, regard, and devotion to that Image. I am devoted to uncovering and developing Divine Love within my being. Love is that quality that grows through giving. I make a habit of giving love to myself to develop my feelings, images, and thoughts for my Divine Purpose. I refuse to believe that thoughts of dislike, abhorrence, and malice are necessary. I accept thoughts of like, acceptance, and accord to receive Divine Love. I love myself, as I am made in the Image of Perfection and cannot dwell upon thoughts that do not honor my True Being. I desire to be loved by all. Love is my true nature. I am made from Love, and I call forth love from my feelings, images, and thoughts to receive Divine Love. I appreciate myself; I love myself. As I accept the Image in which I am made, my eyes reflect the beauty of that Image. I stand firm and declare that all feelings must be in support of that Image. I welcome all feelings and call them good and very good. I am unified with my feelings, images, and thoughts and re-establish the bond of love for the Image in which I am made. I court feelings of goodwill, altruism, and charity. I am unselfish in my assessment of my feelings, images, and thoughts. I look for and see the truth in my feelings, images, and thoughts to guide me to the Image in which I am made. I am thankful for this realization.

Physical State: Body/Dis-ease/Appearance   Hay Fever
Emotional State: Soul – tranquility, passion, bliss
Mental State: Mind – rage, grief, sadness
Spiritual State: Law – Peace (undeveloped)

I become quiet and still and have patience with my feelings, images, and thoughts to move through this event in peace. I make wise use of the Image in which I am made and let go of all feelings, images, and thoughts that do not support who I am. I remove the judgment from my feelings, images, and thoughts to express Divine Peace. I am tranquil, filled with fervor to experience ecstasy through my feelings, images, and thoughts. I abstain from entertaining thoughts of rage, grief, and sadness to express Divine Peace. I indulge in and yield to thoughts that are calm, consoling, and soothing. I trust and have confidence in the Image in which I am made to understand this event. I am delighted, pleased, and eager to express Divine Peace. I bring harmony to my feelings, images, and thoughts as I receive Divine Peace. I participate in joyful activities. I delight in expressing Divine Peace. I am brave in my assessment of my feelings, images, and thoughts to move into the Image in which I am made. I am set free from all that is not of love. Love purifies my thinking about myself. Patience allows me to accept all ideas that flow through me to encourage peaceful action. I now take dominion over my feelings, images, and thoughts to reorder my world to establish Divine Peace. I am active and alive. I do not resist life; I embrace Life. I draw upon the Image in which I am made to bring unity into my world of feelings, images, and thoughts. Divine Peace floods my being. Joy fills my world with trust. I am confident as I walk boldly through all situations, knowing that the Image in which I am made transports me into the light of bliss. I am delighted to know that my feelings, images, and thoughts are guiding me to express Divine Peace. I am calm. I give thanks for the privilege to restore my feelings, images, and thoughts to express Divine Peace.

Physical State: Body/Dis-ease/Appearance   Headache
Emotional State: Soul – gratitude, trust, serenity
Mental State: Mind – impatient, stressed, confused
Spiritual State: Law – Peace (undeveloped)

I know that love protects and guards me, and I am guided to pathways of peace. I am filled with confidence as joy fills my being. I move with sureness of speech and action. I live in expectation of an enthusiastic and joy-filled life. Divine Peace now fills me with Joy. In gratitude, trust, and serenity, I assess my feelings, images, and thoughts to express Divine Peace. As such, I refute all thoughts of impatience, stress, and confusion as necessary to express Divine Peace. I accept, dwell upon, and court thoughts that bring serenity, poise, and clarity. My feelings, images, and thoughts are my guideposts to express the Image in which I am made. I face all situations with confidence, thanksgiving, and composure. I have the assurance and clarity to uphold my responsibility to live from that Image. I move with certainty, conviction, and honor to express Divine Peace. I rest in sweet repose. I rely upon, expect, and depend upon my feelings, images, and thoughts to comfort me in this experience. I appreciate who I am. I have faith in the Image in which I am made and have the conviction to express Divine Peace. I call upon and claim my gift of Divine Peace and allow life and love to take place in my world of affairs. My days are filled with joyful activity and my nights are filled with thoughts of peace. I now unify my feelings, images, and thoughts to express as one, in harmony and union. I rest in peace as I participate in Life. I accept the Image in which I am made, knowing I have the courage to fulfill Its every need. I now accept all feelings, images, and thoughts as my tools to experience Divine Peace—that peace that outshines all understanding. I trust in the Image in which I am made and experience vitality and security of Its Infinite Peace. My mind is filled with thoughts of contentment, and I am congenial. I am grateful that Divine Peace prevails in my world.

Physical State: Body/Dis-ease Heart
Emotional State: Soul — passion, rapture, devotion
Mental State: Mind — resentment, escape, rejection
Spiritual State: Law — Love (undeveloped)

Right now, I commit myself to expressing Divine Love. I begin to greet each hour with joy, every person with love, and every seeming difficulty with confidence. Divine Intelligence from the Image in which I am made directs my thoughts, my words, and my deeds. Consequently, I come to know the truth about my body and my life. I call upon the Image in which I am made to comfort me as move through this situation. I now commit myself to expressing passion, rapture, and devotion from the Image in which I am made. I accept ecstasy, elation, and dedication as part of my duty to express Divine Love. I am passionate in my desire to live from the image in which I am made. I am elated. I turn in reverence to the Image in which I am made and relish my understanding of that which I am. I am charitable, loving, and loyal to my feelings, images, and thoughts, and I bring them into concord with who I am. I refuse to dwell upon thoughts of resentment, escape, and rejection. I embrace, claim, and accept thoughts that bring approval, freedom, and acceptance of my feelings, images, and thoughts. I remain steadfast, undaunted, and unmovable in my desire to live from the Image in which I am made. I begin now to look beyond appearances and reshape my life to express Divine Love. I only accept and embrace feelings, images, and thoughts of satisfaction and delight. I revel in my resolve to express Divine Love. I praise myself. I love myself just as I am. I am comforted by this knowledge. I hold my feelings, images, and thoughts in high regard; they are signposts to lead me to the Image in which I am made. I participate in activities that bring joy, filled with pleasure and glee. I have the assurance that as I move boldly and confidently thought this experience, courage and trust are restored. I give thanks and accept complete restoration of my health.

Physical State: Body/Dis-ease/Appearance　Hemorrhoids
Emotional State: Soul – confidence, competence, aptitude
Mental State: Mind – fear, tension, anxiety
Spiritual State: Law – Power (undeveloped)

I am aware of the pulse of Life moving through my feelings, images, and thoughts. Right now I listen. I become teachable, observing Divine Power as it flows through me. I am a firm believer in the efficacy of my feelings, images, and thoughts through my faith in the Image in which I am made. I have the capacity and power of dominion over my life. I have confidence in who I am. I know that I am competent and have the aptitude to express Divine Power. Therefore, I do not accept thoughts of fear, tension, and anxiety as real. I accept only thoughts of bravery, relaxation, and relief as I express Divine Power. I am liberated, relieved, and secure in my assessment of my feelings, images, and thoughts. I am reassured by the Image in which I am made as I resolve to express Divine Power. I feel secure, calm, and carefree in my assessment of my feelings, images, and thoughts. I am peaceful and calm. The vim, vigor, and vitality of the Image in which I am made flow through me to strengthen me to express Divine Power. I am proficient. I have courage. I am brave. I draw upon this power to fill my mind with clear directions. I have the potential to rise above all feelings, images, and thoughts. I am effective in discerning my life. I am courageous in all my actions. Divine Power is my gift. I use my gift rightly in dealing with my feelings, images, and thoughts. I find strength and comfort in determining that which is for my highest good. I claim my power to bring change into my life under the guidance of the Image in which I am made. I have faith that my word is now fulfilled. I claim leadership over my life. I am empowered. I feel relieved. I rejoice in the Image in which I am made. I accept who I am. I am at peace. Divine Power flows freely through me, fulfilling every need. I take stock of my abilities and skills to change my feelings, images, and thoughts to reflect Divine Power. I give thanks.

Physical State: Body/Dis-ease/Appearance   Hernia
Emotional State: Soul – intelligence, sagacity
Mental State: Mind – anger, overload
Spiritual State: Law – Wisdom (undeveloped)

I trust my inner guidance of wisdom. I stand secure in my discernment of my feelings, images, and thoughts to comprehend the purpose of this event. I am content with the knowledge that I am made in the Image and likeness of Perfection. Therefore, I use prudence, foresight, and Intelligence to restore my health to express Divine Wisdom. I refuse to believe this event is necessary to express Divine Wisdom. I accept, affirm, and court thoughts that are loving, calm, and soothing to express Divine Wisdom. I am relieved. I let go and allow the flow of Divine Wisdom to flow though me. I am confident, efficient, and have the capacity to express Divine Wisdom. I trust the Image in which I am made to guide me through this experience. I have the aptitude, appreciation, and respect for my feelings, images, and thoughts to express Divine Wisdom. I am relaxed and at ease. I use good judgment in assessing my feelings, images, and thoughts to express Divine Wisdom. I am content. I allow the wisdom in my feelings, images, and thoughts to guide me to my highest desire to express Divine Wisdom. I am satisfied with who I am. I expand my thoughts to include Divine Wisdom. I am patient with myself. I am fulfilled. I have a calm endurance that frees me from all feelings, images, and thoughts unlike my true nature. My true nature is Divine. I am motivated, inspired, and consoled by the Image in which I am made. I embrace this experience in joy as I now know the purpose is to express Divine Wisdom. I relax. I am safe. I love myself just the way I am. I am that light unto myself, and I use that light to restore my health in this event. I am unmoved by anything or anyone outside of me, as my power comes from the Image in which I am made. I recognize the power within every feeling, image, and thought and use that power for good. I give thanks for the feelings, images, and thoughts as they are restored to express Divine Power.

Physical State: Body/Dis-ease   Hip
Emotional State: Soul — endurance, tolerance
Mental State: Mind — pain, fear, anxiety
Spiritual State: Law — Joy (undeveloped)

I now bring my feelings, images, and thoughts in alignment with the Image in which I am made. I claim my freedom from all events that limit me from expressing Divine Joy. I feel secure in making decisions to express Divine Joy from the Image in which I am made. I rely upon and I am faithful to the purpose of experiencing pleasure and joy in all circumstances. I am now convinced that I have the endurance and tolerance to express Divine Joy. I respect my feelings, images, and thoughts to guide me. I am free to express Divine Joy. I refute all thoughts of pain, fear and anxiety as necessary to experience Divine Joy. I accept only thoughts of relief, bravery, and assurance to move through this event to express Divine Joy. I take delight and solace in knowing the Image in which I am made supports me in my resolve to express Divine Joy. I draw upon tenacity, stability and stamina to express Divine Joy. I have fortitude and perseverance to see myself through all situations. I remain steadfast and unmovable in living from the Image in which I am made. I am relieved. I am patient in my understanding of myself and submissive to the flow of Life that I am. I cooperate with the Image in which I am made. I am now willing to allow my thoughts to produce the effects necessary to live from the Image in which I am made. I am supportive and genuine in my effort to live from the Image in which I am made. I am tolerant in my understanding of all feelings, images, and thoughts. I am at peace. I welcome any and all opportunities to express Divine Joy in all my activities. I am now on my path to full and wondrous freedom from all judgments of my feelings, images, and thoughts of separation. I sustain in my heart the love to forgive, the wisdom to understand, and the peace to forebear. I live courageously, joyously, and at ease as I express from the Image in which I am made. I give thanks.

Physical State: Body/Affairs/Appearance   Hope (lack of)
Emotional State: Soul — endurance, vitality
Mental State: Mind — belief, trust, courage
Spiritual State: Law — Life (undeveloped)

I praise the Image in which I am made. I am made in the Image of Perfection; therefore, I have all that I need to sustain my life. I am optimistic about life. I have the ability to withstand without bending. I am revitalized when I look on the brighter side of this experience. I move with certainty from the Image in which I am made. I change my belief to trust and courage. I am confident in that Image to come forth as I am. I refute all thoughts of unbelief, distrust, and discouragement. I embrace and court thoughts of Truth, assurance, and confidence. I am assured by the image in which I am made of my innate ability to live my life in peace and harmony. I accept feelings of expectation and probability. I lift my mind to that Image. I am encouraged to move with sureness of step, capable of discerning this event. I now see that the purpose of this and all experiences is to develop the Image in which I am made. I trust that Image to guide me to live a more expanded life. My faith is strengthened. My expectations are high. I move with certainty through all feelings, images, and thoughts that strengthen Divine Life. My heart is comforted. I have the incentive to create Divine Life through this experience. I respond to life in love. The Image in which I am made expresses through me. I am filled with the essence of Life. I am filled with vitality. My mental outlook is clear. I hold my life in high regard. My assessment of this event is sound. I draw upon the wellspring of Wisdom within to generate new feelings, images, and thoughts about my life. I love Life.

Physical State: Body/Affairs   Hypocrisy
Emotional State: Soul – honesty, authenticity, truth
Mental State: Mind – deceitful, deceptive, false
Spiritual State: Law – Power (undeveloped)

I am the only Power in my life. I draw upon my inner strength to do that which I know to do. I draw upon this power to fill my mind with clear directions. I am courageous in all my actions. The Power from my feelings, images, and thoughts rise up to move me back into the Image in which I am made. Divine Power is my gift and I use my gift wisely. I am true to myself. I am honest and genuine in assessing my feelings, images, and thoughts. I tell myself the truth. I refuse to believe thoughts of deceit, deception and falsehood as necessary to express Divine Power. I claim only thoughts of honesty, sincerity and truth to fashion my life to allow Divine Power to flow through me. I am fair in my assessment of my feelings, images, and thoughts to experience Divine Power. I am forthright in my actions. I am trustworthy. I clear my mind to allow Divine Power to flow through me to change my perception of events in my life. I remove judgment from my feelings, images, and thoughts. I am firm in my decision to uncover Divine Power and use it for the good. I am at peace. I dwell upon thoughts of peace to bring the truth of my being and all others into light. I seize thoughts that support the Image in which I am made. I am open and receptive to thoughts of truth, honesty and uprightness. I have the capacity to govern my feelings, images, and thoughts and as such, I am tolerant in my understanding. I find comfort in using my gift of power for good. I rejoice in ideas that help me live my life from Divine power. I am grateful for this realization of the truth, and it is done.

Physical State: Body/Dis-ease/Appearance   Impotence
Emotional State: Soul – authority, capacity
Mental State: Mind – fear, frustration
Spiritual State: Law – Power (undeveloped)

I acknowledge any and all appearances in my body and have respect for my feelings, images, and thoughts to guide me. I listen and I obey. Appearances change. Truth does not change. I receive Divine Wisdom from the Image in which I am made. Therefore, I have the authority and capacity to restore my body to live from the Image in which I am made. I am conscious of my eternal sufficiency. I determine what is important in my life and refuse to accept fear and frustration as real. I accept thoughts of bravery and encouragement as I satisfy the desire to live from the Image in which I am made. I forgive myself for judgments placed upon this situation and embrace myself in love, fortitude and confidence. I am filled with vim, vigor and vitality that flow from the Image in which I am made. I am tranquil and serene. I am energetic as I participate in life. I tell myself the truth. I persist in living from the Image in which I am made and therefore, I open up to receive Divine Power. Divine Power is my inheritance from the Image in which I am made, and I welcome this opportunity. I accept my responsibility to live a rich and full life. My way is made clear. I trust my feelings, images, and thoughts to guide me in my decision to live from the Image in which I am made. I am unique. I now let go of any tendency to underestimate my capabilities. I have the fortitude to cultivate my feelings, images and thought to demonstrate Divine Power over this event. I free my mind to think only thoughts that produce Divine Power. I depend upon the Image in which I am made to guide me. I have the power to change anything in my life that I do not want to experience and I change my feelings, images, and thoughts right now to express Divine Power. I now use the liberty, love, and power within to restore my body to express Divine Power. In gratitude for this new way of thinking, I relax.

Physical State: Body/Dis-ease/Appearance   Incontinence
Emotional State: Soul – devotion, commitment
Mental State: Mind – weariness, guilt
Spiritual State: Law – Peace (undeveloped)

I center my attention upon Reality. I open my thoughts to the influx of Divine Intelligence and my heart to the warmth of Divine Peace. I turn my attention from appearances and direct it to the Image in which I am made. I know the serenity that accomplishes an all-pervading peace in my world. My heart remains untroubled. My mind is at rest. I trust in the Image in which I am made. I now clear my mind for devotion and commitment to the Image in which I am made. I am loyal to myself and I tell myself the truth. I refute weariness and guilt as real. I accept only thoughts that are vibrant and innocent in context to move into the Image in which I am made. I call a truce to my feelings, images, and thoughts to understand the purpose of this event. I move into harmony with the Image in which I am made and become calm, serene and tranquil. I am energetic, strong and stable in my participation of Life. I am exonerated. I take action upon this event and change this appearance. All appearances are for me to live from the Image in which I am made. I have dominion over appearances in my life, and I take dominion over my feelings, images, and thoughts right now. I embrace all feelings, images, and thoughts, removing the judgment and call it good, and very good. I feel secure, protected and certain of my feelings as I radiate Divine Peace. My feelings, images, and thoughts assure me of my agreement with the Image in which I am made to express Divine Peace. I now understand the purpose of my feelings, images, and thoughts and praise them. I praise, exalt and commend myself in my ability to in express Divine Peace. I love myself. I forgive myself. I admire and approve of who I am. I submit to all feelings, images, and thoughts as I direct them to the Image in which I am made. I now take dominion and emit the essence of Divine Peace to all. I give thanks for my freedom to express Divine Peace.

Physical State: Body/Dis-ease/Appearance   Indigestion
Emotional State: Soul – tranquility, serenity, patience
Mental State: Mind – futility, anxiety, insecurity
Spiritual State: Law – Wisdom (undeveloped)

In this moment, I am content with the knowledge of who I am. I seek Divine Joy in discovering who I am. I use foresight, prudence and astuteness in making all decisions about my life. I am successful in all undertakings. I seek to know the Image in which I am made and as such, tranquility, serenity and patience are the results. I am at peace, calm, and determined to live from the Image in which I am made. I view all events as good and very good. I refuse to entertain thoughts of futility, anxiety, or insecurity. I affirm, court, and embrace thoughts that are effective, comforting, and secure. I remove all judgments from my feelings, images, and thoughts, as they are my tools to direct me as I seek to express Divine Wisdom. I am content. I have everything within me to satisfy all desires to live from the Image in which I am made. I accept thoughts that are cheerful, and loving. Thoughts that relieve fill my mind. I rest in sweet repose. I am consistent in my effort to express Divine Wisdom. I feel secure. I use good judgment, foresight and discernment in my assessment of my feelings, images, and thoughts. I am gentle with myself. I love myself and forgive myself for all judgments placed on my feelings, images, and thoughts. I have the assurance from the Image in which I am made in expressing Divine Wisdom. I am satisfied with who I am. I expand my thoughts to include Divine Wisdom. I am nourished, sustained and provided for by the Image in which I am made. I am wise, sapient and judicious in discerning my feelings, I allow the Image in which I am made to guide me. I listen. I obey and I take action upon thoughts that come to me. I continue in thought as I remember my purpose in this event is to express Divine Wisdom. Divine Wisdom floods my mind and I am free. In thanksgiving and praise for the fullness of life and the ability to express Divine Love, it is done.

Physical State: Body/Dis- ease/Appearance   Infection
Emotional State: Soul – mercy, grace, virtue
Mental State: Mind – hostility, suspicion, annoyance
Spiritual State: Law – Peace (undeveloped)

I let go of old fears and know with sure knowledge, I am forever safe, guided, and protected by the Image in which I am made. I let go of old thought patterns that keep me from the knowledge that I am made in the Image of Perfection. I am alive with the fullness of life from within. I allow Divine Peace to function through me as perfect health. I do not deny the appearance and facts of this appearance; however, I do deny its necessity. I look at appearances as no things, no substance, and, therefore, I see the truth. I change the appearance now with words of power and of truth. The essence of compassion, love and honesty flows through me from the Image in which I am made. Hostility, suspicion and annoyance are no longer part of my thought patterns. I replace all thoughts with peace. I am kind, open to receive and trust the Image in which I am made. I am honest, tender and forgiving of my feelings, images, and thoughts as I view this event as a means to express Divine Peace. I cooperate with the Image in which I am made. I accept divine guidance. I am tolerant, confident and devoted to expressing Divine Peace from the Image in which I am made. I bring harmony, serenity and accord into my world of feelings, images, and thoughts. I nurture myself, bless myself and love myself just as I am. I am patient with myself in my judgments of my feelings, images, and thoughts. I am enthusiastic as I approve of all feelings, images, and thoughts and call them good. All feelings, images, and thoughts lead me to the Image in which I am made. I embrace my feelings with tenderness and sweetness. I comply with them to express Divine Joy. I embrace my feelings, images, and thoughts with fondness, regard, and admiration. I have complete faith in myself to express Divine Peace. I open my heart to its own peace and receive all that I need to express Divine Peace.

Physical State: Body/Dis-ease/Appearance   Inflammation
Emotional State: Soul – mercy, endurance
Mental State: Mind – rage, anger, fear
Spiritual State: Law – Peace (undeveloped)

I observe all thoughts and rejoice as I bring them into the Image in which I am made. I am peaceful now that I know the Purpose for this experience. Feelings, images, and thoughts remind me of who I am. I now dwell upon thoughts that comply with the Image in which I am made. I am patient with myself in judging my feelings, images, and thoughts and receive the good in them for fortitude, tranquility and courage. I can feel as deeply and as intensely as I need to express Divine Peace. I dwell upon thoughts that are pleasant and of gratitude. Love flows from the Image in which I am made to move me through all events in peace. Therefore, I refuse to believe rage, anger and fear are necessary to express Divine Peace. I make firm in my mind thoughts of joy, forgiveness and trust. I have the tenacity, confidence, and compassion to express Divine Peace. I am resolute in my desire to live from the Image in which I am made. I am at peace. I remove all judgment from my assessment of my feelings, images, and thoughts. I am gentle with myself. I am kind to myself. I am filled with joy as I express Divine Peace. I dwell upon feelings of bravery and stability as I express Divine Peace. Each day my body is renewed and I am alive with Divine Peace that flows from the Image in which I am made. I allow Divine Perfection to function through me as Divine Peace. I am active and alive. I do not resist life; I embrace Life and draw upon the Image in which I am made to bring unity into my feelings, images, and thoughts. I accept this event to express Divine Peace. I calm myself. Patience brings understanding to my mind. I am still. I accept the Image in which I am made as who I am. I now sense perfection within me. All evidence of dis-ease is erased by the Image in which I am made. I relax. I am at peace. This is the truth about my body right now.

Physical State: Body/Dis-ease/Appearance   Injuries
Emotional State: Soul – discernment, harmony, tranquility
Mental State: Mind – guilt, anger, suffering
Spiritual State: Law – Peace (undeveloped)

I now embrace my feelings, images, and thoughts to express Divine Peace through the Image in which I am made. I accept right action taking place to restore the Image in which I am made. I am sincere in my resolve to express Divine Peace and call a truce between my feelings, images, and thoughts. I observe my feelings, images, and thoughts with consistent concord and bring harmony, honesty and unity in my assessment. I refuse to believe guilt, anger and suffering is necessary to express Divine Peace. I accept innocent, gleeful and joyous thoughts to dwell upon and court daily. I bring my feelings, images, and thoughts in agreement with my Purpose to express Divine Peace. I am quiet, serene and calm. I am loving, truthful, and sincere in dealing with my feelings, images, and thoughts. I reconcile myself to express Divine Peace in all my activities. I am at ease. I am serene, calm and content. I unify my feelings, images, and thoughts to express from the Image in which I am made and the power is in these words that I speak. I praise my mind, body and soul as it is the vehicle of the Image in which I am made. I move with confidence, freedom and order in expressing from the Image in which I am made. I live in a tranquil atmosphere and clear thinking becomes easy. It is my duty to express Divine Peace in all events in my life and I begin right now. I love and approve of myself. I love and approve of all others. I feel sure of every decision as all ideas flow from the Image in which I am made. My acceptance of these ideas is assimilated as they flow from the Image in which I am made. I affirm and emphatically assert that my feelings, images, and thoughts guide me in knowing and realizing the Image in which I am made. I accept these words to be the truth about the Image in which I am made. In quiet assurance, praise, and thanksgiving, it is done.

Physical State: Body/Dis-ease/Appearance   Insanity
Emotional State: Soul – symmetry, congruence, unity
Mental State: Mind – escape, loneliness, alienation
Spiritual State: Law – Beauty (undeveloped)

I am surrounded by the mystery of Life, which manifests Itself in the clouds, mountains, trees and all of nature. I see beauty. I take time to appreciate the majesty and beauty of Life and learn to live nobly from the Image in which I am made. I am involved in the totality of life. I am rejuvenated in body and mind as I joyfully accept the wholeness of the Image in which I am made. I praise this experience, which gives me the fullness of life to be thankful and grateful for the Image in which I am made. I have all that I need to face any situation that confronts me, and I handle every situation easily and successfully. I look through the veil of confusion, which is about me, and know that I can change my view to harmonize my world. My feelings, images, and thoughts are my tools to guide me and I take away all judgment to express Divine Beauty from the Image in which I am made. I bring my feelings, images, and thoughts in alignment to experience balance, agreement and oneness with the Image in which I am made. I disprove thoughts of escape, loneliness and alienation as necessary to express Divine Beauty. I approve, embrace, and dwell upon thoughts that liberate, honor and unite to express Divine Beauty. I am never alone as the Image in which I am made is forever present. I accept only feelings, images, and thoughts of praise, approval and encouragement to express Divine Beauty. I am loved, cherished and honored by the Image in which I am made. I am balanced. I love myself just as I am. I appreciate who I am. I am competent, sane and poised in evaluating my feelings, images, and thoughts. I am gentle with myself. All feelings, images, and thoughts are worthwhile, steady and deliberate for the purpose of expressing Divine Beauty in this event. I welcome the opportunity to express Divine Beauty and give thanks for the realization of its purpose.

Physical State: Body/Dis-ease/Appearance   **Insomnia**
Emotional State: Soul – trust, faith, fidelity
Mental State: Mind – worry, anxiety, guilt
Spiritual State: Law – Peace (undeveloped)

I am of good cheer as I accept my purpose to express Divine Peace in this experience. I look through the eyes of praise, wisdom and love. I am competent, qualified and have the capacity to live from the Image in which I am made. I trust who I am. I have credence and faith in who I am as I devote myself to expressing Divine Peace. I inquire of my feelings, images, and thoughts to guide me in this experience. My feelings, images, and thoughts are harmless and I can discern that which truth is for me. I praise, laude, and approve of all feelings, images, and thoughts, removing the judgment of disbelief. I refuse to believe worry, anxiety and guilt as necessary to express Divine Peace. I maintain to be true all feelings, images, and thoughts of comfort, assurance and innocence. I court feelings images and thoughts of credence, belief and devotion as the foundation for the Image in which I am made to express Divine Peace in this experience. I am steadfast, responsible and loyal to the Image in which I am made. I am reassured that my security is in the Image in which I am made. My feelings, images, and thoughts are now calm, filled with promise and honor. I am consistent in my charge to express Divine Peace. I am responsible to the Image in which I am made to express Divine Peace and this experience is one that affords the opportunity. I seize it with joy, enthusiasm and faith. I view my feelings, images, and thoughts with accuracy and precision and rely upon them to guide me to the Image in which I am made. I have the certainty of that Image to succeed. I am reassured in my efforts to express Divine Peace. I praise all situations, events and conditions in my life, using discrimination in assessing every feeling, image and thought. I love myself; I praise myself and rejoice in this experience to express Divine Peace. I now sleep in peace, and awake refreshed, giving thanks for this realization.

Physical State: Body/Dis-ease   Intestines
Emotional State: Soul – ecstasy exultation, rapture
Mental State: Mind – pain, sorrow, grief
Spiritual State: Law – Life (undeveloped)

I commend myself for my ability to discern my feelings, images, and thoughts and accept them as real and natural. I let go of my opinion of facts and move into the truth of the Image in which I am made. I give myself to the clear vision and wisdom of the Image in which I am made and tell myself the truth. Truth removes all confusion. I am now opened to pure Ideas from the Image in which I am made. I remove self-imposed blindness and draw upon that Image to restore my body to express Divine Life. I accept the out pouring of ecstasy as I am exalted to experience rapture. I revel in this opportunity to express Divine Life. I am triumphant. I am delighted to know that this experience allows me to express Divine Life and that I am at peace. I refuse to grant feelings, images, and thoughts of pain, sorrow and grief entrance into my world as I ratify only thoughts of joy, comfort and gladness to take root and grow. I find satisfaction, contentment and pleasure in expressing Divine Life. I seek activity that brings merriment to express Divine Life. I no longer fight false beliefs; I accept the truth about the Image in which I am made and I have the power to succeed. My feelings, images, and thoughts assure me of my aliveness: I nurture my feelings, images, and thoughts with love and rely upon them to lead me to belief and faith. I am reassured of life by my feelings, images, and thoughts. Life is activity and I participate in my life. I draw upon the vitality of life. I have the endurance, courage and stamina to conduct my feelings, images, and thoughts in a manner to express Divine Life. I am now conscious of the Image in which I am made to lead, guide and direct me through this experience. The Image in which I am made is the healing presence to restore my feelings, images, and thoughts to the original perfection. I praise myself. I reward myself. I rejoice that I know who I am, and my purpose is to express Divine Life in this experience. I am grateful.

Physical State: Body/Dis- ease/Appearance   Itching
Emotional State: Soul – faith, trust, hope
Mental State: Mind – anxiety, fear, guilt
Spiritual State: Law – Peace (undeveloped)

I am worthy to live from the Image in which I am made. I draw upon the courage, valor and fortitude to express Divine Peace. I have reverence for my feelings, images, and thoughts and so order my thinking to express Divine Peace. My mind is now open and my expectation is high for my heart's desire to fulfill life. I desire to rise to the Image in which I am made to lead, guide, and direct me to express Divine Peace. That peace becomes my peace of mind. I listen. I obey. This experience affords me the opportunity to express Divine Peace from the Image in which I am made. Everything I do is a beginning of a new life. I now commit myself to dwell in the Image in which I am made for it is definite and my conviction is firm. I have faith, trust and hope to inspire me to live from that Image. Therefore I deny anxiety, fear and guilt as necessary to express Divine Peace. I make firm in my mind thoughts of ease, daring and freedom to express Divine Peace. I am confident that I have all that I need to fulfill my desire to express Divine Peace from the Image in which I am made. I am calm, trusting and reliable. I endeavor to change my feelings, images, and thoughts to reflect Divine Order, as I assert myself to trust in the Image in which I am made. I live in expectancy. I am adequate for the task. I am content. I stand firm upon feelings of peace, quiet and that which brings serenity. I accept my feelings, images, and thoughts as a reminder of my conviction to express Divine Peace. I am at one, agreeable and serene with all feelings, images, and thoughts. I remove the misjudgments and accept myself just as I am. I have complete faith and trust in my ability to restore my world to express Divine Peace. I live from my true nature – the Image in which I am made. I now view this event as an opportunity to express Divine Peace from the Image in which I am made. I now give thanks, resting in thoughts of peace, as I let it be.

Physical State: Body/Dis-ease   Jaw
Emotional State: Soul — discernment, mercy, tranquility
Mental State: Mind — rage, revenge, anger
Spiritual State: Law — Power (undeveloped)

I was created in the Image and likeness of Perfection to enjoy life in peace that brings pleasure in living from the Image in which I am made. I identify with, accept and live a creative, fun filled life. I rise above this event and draw upon feelings, images, and thoughts to express Divine Power. I now distinguish my images, feelings and thoughts from all that do not support me in expressing Divine Power. I rejoice as I experience mercy and tranquility from the Image in which I am made. I am sensible, sagacious and compassionate in observing my feelings, images, and thoughts. I abstain from thinking thoughts of rage, revenge and anger as I draw upon thoughts that confirm composure, pardon and reasonable thinking. I am gentle and tolerant with my feelings, images, and thoughts, as they are my guides for living from the Image in which I am made. I think clearly, my perception is keen and my actions are sure. I have the endurance to move thought this event to express Divine Power. I stand firm upon my resolve and absolve myself of all judgments placed on my feelings, images, and thoughts. I have the strength, capacity and capability to live from the Image in which I am made. I draw upon my inner resources to express Divine Power. My ability, skill and talent rise up from the Image in which I am made and Divine Power flows through me. I have the supremacy, sovereignty and mastery over my feelings, images, and thoughts to express Divine Power. I have been given the government to so order my world of feelings, images, and thoughts to radiate Divine Power. I love myself. I approve of myself just the way I am as I am made in the Image and likeness of Perfection. I am certain of this truth as it unfolds in my world of thought. I am at peace. Divine Power rises up within me and restores my body to express from the Image in which I am made. For this knowing, I give thanks. And so it is.

Physical State: Body/Affairs   Jealousy
Emotional State: Soul – trusting, enthused, caring
Mental State: Mind – suspicious, dubious, covetousness
Spiritual State: Law - Life (undeveloped)

I am honorable in my intent to uncover the essence of Life through my feelings, images, and thoughts. I am faithful and true to my intent. I face this experience squarely. I seek the righteousness of it. I am unique. I grasp this experience to understand my true purpose. I trust the Image in which I am made and therefore, generous in my assessment of my feelings, images, and thoughts. I refuse to believe thoughts of suspicion, dubiousness, and covetousness to experience Divine Life. I affirm I have the confidence that I am enough. I am open to new experiences and see this event clearly. I am sure of my ability to uncover the Image in which I am made and depend upon myself to bring that Image to the Light. I am dependable, trustworthy and definite in my effort to heal my mind of thoughts that do not support the Image in which I am made. I aspire to understand my feelings, images, and thoughts. I am selfless, enthused, and generous in my assessment of my Life. Divine Life flowing through me lifts me to heights of Joy. My desire is to know who I am, and my feelings, images, and thoughts are my guides to that knowing. I court feelings of trust, credence and faith. I elevate my mind to accept my feelings, images, and thoughts. Life is eternal. There is no cessation of Life. My desire is to express Divine Life. I seek my own. I have enough. I am enough. The Image in which I am made is uncovered and I embrace myself in love. Divine Life is my gift and I accept it now.

Physical State: Body/Dis-ease   Joints
Emotional State: Soul – endurance, discretion, illumination
Mental State: Mind – resentment, suppression
Spiritual State: Law – Wisdom (undeveloped)

I surrender to the Image in which I am made. I am modest in my assessment of my feelings, images, and thoughts and remove all judgment placed upon them. I am important to this world as I approach life in a simple manner, praising the Image in which I am made. I am humbled. I am unpretentious in my judgment and bring forth the dignity of the Image in which I am made. I am worthy to receive Divine Wisdom and open up to receive renewed feelings, images, and thoughts to claim my true self worth. I court consideration of my feelings, gentleness in my speech and patience in my thought to express Divine Wisdom. I have the support, acuteness, and foresight in my interpretation of my feelings, images, and thoughts. I welcome the opportunity to revel the Image in which I am made. I am illumined. I refute feelings, images, and thoughts of resentment and suppression as I vindicate, support and confirm thoughts of approval and expression of Divine Wisdom. I have the courage, ability and clarification of the purpose of this event to express Divine Wisdom. I am worthy. I am capable. I am effective. I am inspired by clear thinking and sound reasoning. I praise myself to bring out the gentleness within me. I am eager to experience the Image in which I am made. I am relaxed as I feel the flow of Divine Wisdom. I utilize my feelings, images, and thoughts to bring me to Divine Wisdom in my entire decision making processes. My thoughts produce my feelings and images to express Divine Wisdom. I am successful. I am useful. I am wise. I draw upon my understanding of the Image in which I am made to bring out the essence of Divine Wisdom for expression in my life. My reasoning is clear thinking. My understanding is sound. My thoughts are elevated. My perception is keen. I approve of myself. I love myself. I accept the truth of me through this experience.

Physical State: Body/Affairs Joy
Emotional State: Soul — ecstasy, exultation, rapture
Mental State: Mind — glee, felicity, awe
Spiritual State: Law — Joy (undeveloped)

I find pleasure in entertaining ideas of joy and cheerful things to do. Everything I need to support me in my desire to express Divine Joy is within my feelings, images, and thoughts. I delight in participating in Life. I am joyful in uncovering my feelings, images, and thoughts to reveal the Image in which I am made. My Spirit is high. I am exhilarated. I court thoughts of glee, felicity and awe to transport me to the place to experience Divine Joy. There is no place for sadness, unhappiness or misery in my life as my desire is to experience Divine Joy. I am effective in my efforts to uncover the Image in which I am made. I accept this Divine Gift and I am in awe of its magnificence. I now call upon feelings of rapture and glee to enhance the flow of Divine Joy. I receive from Life all that makes me joyful and content. This moment I seek my union with Life. I withdraw the veils that hide my true nature and thereby unveil the Reality of my life. I allow my inward nature to penetrate all feelings, images, and thoughts to uncover the Image in which I am made. Divine Joy increases my capacity to love unconditionally. My appreciation of it gives and promotes kindness. I welcome every opportunity to uncover my life to reveal Divine Joy. I enter into the fullness of joy that is mine by the Image in which I am made. I am constantly aware of my inner prompting to experience Divine Joy. I choose to be true to the best that is in me. This is my birthright. Joy confirms my faith. Joy dominates my moods. I joyously anticipate experiences of rapture and exultation. I am transported to the Image in which I am made.

Physical State: Body/Dis-ease   Kidney
Emotional State: Soul – mercy, solitude, enlightenment
Mental State: Mind – critical, lonely, confused
Spiritual State: Law – Peace (undeveloped)

I have assurance from the Image in which I am made as I move boldly and confidently though this experience. Courage and trust are my guides. I open up to receive mercy, solitude, and enlightenment from the Image in which I am made. I seek cheerful and happy feelings, images, and thoughts to fulfill my life. I become still, this very moment to allow Divine Peace to flow through me. I abstain from indulging in thoughts producing disorder, ill health, mental anxiety through critical, lonely and confused thinking. I persist and continue to indulge in thoughts of order, perfect health, and mental clarity. I court feelings, images, and thoughts that are complimentary, sociable and clarity to live from the Image in which I am made. I remove all judgment placed upon this event and unify myself in feeling, images and thought to draw upon the creative power of Divine Peace. I am in my right place. Trust courage and order now come into my feelings, actions and thoughts. I now establish my life to conform to my conviction to live from the Image in which I am made. Each experience is a divine appointment to live from the Image in which I am made, and this one is to express Divine Peace. I gain a sense of serenity and contentment. Methods to accomplish tasks for completion are shown to me. I am at peace as I assess my feelings, images, and thoughts. Divine Peace soothes, gratifies and pleases me. I am emotionally stable, competent and undaunted in my efforts to live from the fullness of the Image in which I am made. Divine Peace floods my world. I stand guard at the doorway of my thoughts, refusing entrance to anything that is not of love, joy and peace. I unify and accept my feelings, images, and thoughts to express Divine Peace. I am in agreement with who I am. I rest in sweet repose and praise who I am. I love myself. Joyously, I align myself with the Image in which I am made.

Physical State: Body/Affairs   Kindness
Emotional State: Soul – compassion, empathy, gentleness
Mental State: Mind – unkind, harsh, severe
Spiritual State: Law – Joy (undeveloped)

I am aware, alert and awake, filled with strength, enthusiasm and glee. I give freely and Joyfully to Life and I receive from Life all that makes me free to live from the Image in which I am made. I am understanding, gracious and considerate in assessing my feelings, images, and thoughts. I am in perfect harmony and accord with my life. I give myself unstintingly to Life. This I do spontaneously and with Joy. I am compassionate, empathetic and handled my feelings, images, and thoughts with gentleness and care. I love myself just as I am. I accept myself just as I am. I am gentle with myself. I refute thoughts that are unkind, harsh and severe as I embrace thoughts of insistent, meekness and tolerant of who I am. I am consistent and undeviating in my action to bring forth Divine Joy. I give myself attention. I take time to manage my life. I receive pleasure in my life. Joy is bountiful. I give thanks for the gift of Life and for my capacity to give and receive love. I am generous in my assessment of my feelings, images, and thoughts. I feel unified. I am aware of acts of kindness to bring peace of mind. I am inspired; I seek the good and find it in all actions. I revel in pure delight as I uncover my feelings, images, and thoughts and Divine Joy is revealed. I take time to appreciate the majesty and splendor of Life and accept only good as my Divine Right. I am involved with the totality of Life. I am thankful for the knowledge of the Image in which I am made. I participate in my life to bring forth Kindness to my actions. I rejoice in this experience.

Physical State: Body/Dis-ease   Knee
Emotional State: Soul – endurance, tolerance, humility
Mental State: Mind – stubborn, obstinate, insecure
Spiritual State: Law – Power (undeveloped)

I do all that I can to enjoy my Life. Right now, I stop blaming myself for behaviors made in ignorance of Divine Power. I no longer do things that make me unhappy just so others can feel good. I now take charge of my feelings, images, and thoughts to bring out and live from the image in which I am made. I have the stamina, patience and humility to express Divine Power. I refute feelings, images, and thoughts of stubbornness, obstinacy, and insecurity as necessary to express Divine Power. I ratify, accept, and embrace thoughts that are patient, compliant, and safe to express Divine Power. I now know that this experience is to guide me to the Image in which I am made .I am trustworthy, stable and have the fortitude to move through this and all experience. I have the strength, resilience and confident to live from the Image in which I am made. I am versatile in my movements, enduring this event as one to express Divine Power. I submit to the Image in which I am made. I persevere, bravely to my freedom to express Divine Power. I change my feelings, images, and thoughts to comply with the Image in which I am made. My thoughts come to guide me to the Image in which I am made. I forgive myself. I commend myself. My body and mind are tools to help me live joyously, lovingly and freely in the Image in which I am made. I am liberated from feelings, images, and thoughts that stand in the way of my fully knowing the Image in which I am made. I respect my feelings, images, and thoughts for the message I receive to express Divine Power. I love myself. I now see and understand this appearance as necessary to draw me closer to the Image in which I am made. Ideas come to restore my feelings, images, and thoughts to move forward with grace and ease. I am flexible in my movements. In thanksgiving and quiet confidence, I live from my true nature and express Divine Power through this and all experiences.

Physical State: Body/Affairs   Knowing
Emotional State: Soul — discerning, wise, sound
Mental State: Mind — idle, unwise, unintelligent
Spiritual State: Law — Wisdom (undeveloped)

I know all that I need to know whenever I need to know it. That which is within me knows that it knows, and I order my thinking to receive from that part of me. I have the ability to discern my life and any situation in which I encounter with wisdom and sound thinking. I refuse to believe that idleness, unwise decisions and unintelligent thought as necessary for me to receive Divine Wisdom. I declare, contend and claim productive thought processes, wise decision making and intelligent ideas flow through my mind at all times. I am made in the Image and Likeness of Perfection; therefore, I have the foresight, capacity and depth of knowledge to uncover the Image in which I am made. I have good skills and use my mind for inspiration and reasoning. I think clearly, with precision and insight. I receive the facts and information to experience Divine Wisdom. Divine Wisdom is my heritage. I have the ability to know. I am wise. Good judgment supports me in all decision making. I am enlightened by the Image in which I am made to move through this experience in grace and ease. I love myself. I am thoughtful. I am intelligent and well versed in any event in which I participate. I assess my feelings, images, and thoughts with Divine Wisdom. Intelligence comes from the Image in which I am made, and I now realize who I am and move through this event in peace. I am free to feel, think and speak from the Image in which I am made as the fountain of Divine Wisdom overflows within me. I am grateful for this and all experiences that bring me closer to knowing who I am.

Physical State: Body/Dis-ease   Knuckle
Emotional State: Soul – transformation
Mental State: Mind – pain, stiffness, tautness
Spiritual State: Law – Peace (undeveloped)

I permit Divine Peace to fill me. Therefore I relax and know that I am bathed in pure love and everlasting Peace. I no longer resist who I am. I rejoice in knowing the Image in which I am made. Appearances are not real and this event is an appearance, supportive of my resolve to live from the image in which I am made. I stand firm that the Life within me is of spontaneous love. I do everything with ease and joy. I embrace Life. I have such a complete sense of my union with life that with change I receive pleasure. I abstain from indulging in images, feelings, and thoughts of pain, stiffness and tautness. I confirm thoughts of comfort, flexibility, and freedom. That which I am is Life Itself, stimulating every feeling, image and thought to a joyful, peaceful and successful accomplishment. I feel secure in who I am. I elevate my thought world to experience ecstasy. I live an enthusiastic life of creative joy, finding complete self-expression in everything I do. My feelings, images, and thoughts are now unified to express Divine Peace. I am honest in my desire to express Divine Peace. I alter, adjust and replace all thoughts that do not harmonize with my purpose to live from the Image in which I am made. I find relief when I yield to that Image. I am now conscious of my union with the Image in which I am made. My values are sound, honest and fair. I have an awareness of myself as whole and happy. A sense of peace, adequacy and power fills my being. This moment, I willingly change my feelings, images, and thoughts to support my conversion to the Image in which I am made. I yield to it. I am free. I adjust my life to move forward thought this experience to express Divine Peace. I love myself. I am at peace with myself. I find pleasure and delight in expressing Divine Peace. I complete all tasks with ease and joy. I accept the Image in which I am made as who I am. I free myself to live in Divine Peace.

Physical State: Body/Dis-ease/Appearance   Laryngitis
Emotional State: Soul – rapture, passion, devotion
Mental State: Mind – anger, irritation, resentment
Spiritual State: Law – Love (undeveloped)

Love is the healing power in all appearances, events, experiences, and conditions. I now turn to the Image in which I am made wherein lies all my strength and peace. I am integrated and established in my world beyond questioning. Nothing can take love from me or keep it out of my heart. I now open up for Love to enter freely into my world. I do not ignore the appearance of this condition as I accept all appearances as guides for me to draw upon the Image in which I am made. I open up for the experience of rapture, passion and devotion to unfold in my experience to express Divine Love. I welcome the essence of ecstasy, fervor and attention to flow from the Image in which I am made. I abstain from indulging in feelings, images, and thoughts of anger, irritation, and resentment as necessary to express Divine Love. I indulge in thoughts of love, comfort and approval to restore my world to receive Divine Love. I am attentive to my feelings, images, and thoughts and forgive myself for my judgments of who I say I am. I hold high regard for the Image in which I am made. I take delight in expressing Divine Love. I am accepting of who I am and express Divine Love in joy. I am elated. Pleasure fills every activity. I now know Divine Love seeks Its way through me and I open my heart to receive. I know I am wanted, appreciated and needed to express Divine Love. I declare my love now for the Image in which I am made. I am calm, at ease and rest in sweet repose now that I know my purpose is to express Divine Love. Divine Love accompanies all feelings, images, and thoughts. I dwell upon thoughts of cooperation, compliance and devotion as these thoughts lead me to the Image in which I am made. I have an allegiance to that Image to dwell upon thoughts of expansion and latitude. All thoughts offer the opportunity to receive Divine Love. In praise and thanksgiving, I accept Divine Love in my life right now.

Physical State: Body/Dis-ease   Leg
Emotional State: Soul – reverence, awe, endurance
Mental State: Mind – fear, insecurity, timorousness
Spiritual State: Law – Power (undeveloped)

Right now, I clear my mind to know the truth about my health. I am made in the Image and Likeness of Perfection, therefore, unified, whole and complete. Everything that I need to move through this experience is in the Image in which I am made. There is nothing within me that can hinder or interfere with the emergence of the Image in which I am made. I move with dauntless courage to live from my true nature as made in the Image of Perfection. As such, I have available to me all the assurance and dominion to draw upon. I clear my mind right now to express Divine Power. I open up to experience reverence, awe and endurance from the Image in which I am made. Honor, wonder and stamina are by products to express Divine Power. I reject feelings, images, and thoughts of fear, insecurity and timorous in support of expressing Divine Power. I accept feelings, images, and thoughts of courage, security and confidence as the foundation for my world of thought. I am brave, determined and have the capacity to express Divine Power. I am resolute in moving forward in my decision to live from the Image in which I am made. I have deep respect for the Image in which I am made and take a stand to revere, honor and venerate that which I am. I have the assurance, understanding and capacity to express Divine Power. I am brave, bold and confident in moving into the Image in which I am made. I take dominion over my world and move toward changing all feelings, images, and thoughts to reflect the Image in which I am made. I enlarge and extend my feelings, images, and thoughts to include adoration, admiration and affection for the Image in which I am made. I live and act totally from the image in which I am made to express Divine Power. Divine Love heals. Divine Power uplifts. Divine Peace comforts. I am grateful for this realization of the Image in which I am made, and I allow Divine Power to flow freely though my life.

Physical State: Body/Dis-ease/Appearance   Leukemia
Emotional State: Soul – trust, faith, endurance
Mental State: Mind – depression, anger, despair
Spiritual State: Law – Peace (undeveloped)

Right now, I expect every good thing to come to me. I affirm my union with all Life. Divine Intelligence stimulates everything I do, say, and think. I am necessary for the expression of Divine Peace through the Image in which I am made. Trust, faith and endurance flows from the Image in which I am made and I am revived. I change my belief to one of fidelity and am filled with the vitality of the Image in which I am made. I refuse to believe depression, anger and despair as necessary to express Divine Peace. I affirm, court, and embrace feelings, images, and thoughts of cheer, that are of love and filled with hope. I have the confidence, assurance and credence of the Image in which I am made to move through this experience in peace. I am certain, Divine Peace and joy soothe my mind. I am agreeable, friendly and amiable in my assessment of my feelings, images, and thoughts. I am persuaded to express Divine Peace through this event. I have the conviction to move through this experience in trust and faith. Thanksgiving and appreciation are continually in my thoughts; I am considerate, thoughtful and gentle in expressing Divine Peace. I now know the purpose for this event and I feel secure in my resolve to live from the Image in which I am made. I have the certainty of who I am to express Divine Peace. I have the ability to withstand without bending. I expand my feelings, images, and thoughts to express more of Divine Peace. I am a physical expression of peace. I experience love, naturally and in peace. I am honest in my assessment of my feelings, images, and thoughts and am relieved to know the purpose for this experience is to consciously recognize the Image in which I am made. I am steadfast in my determination to express from the Image in which I am made. I condition my mind to accept Divine Peace. I consciously give thanks for the knowledge of who I am.

Physical State: Body/Affairs   Life
Emotional State: Soul – endurance, vitality, awareness
Mental State: Mind – dispirited, sad, fatigued
Spiritual State: Law – Life (undeveloped)

I now state what I desire from Life and make the conscious decision to live and conduct my life in that manner. I call upon that part of me that is made in the Image and of Perfection to support my decision to Live. I am alert, awake and aware of Life's splendor. I persist in living life to its fullest. I participate in Life. I honor Life. I have the endurance, vitality and Source to live life. That Source is the Image of Perfection. I draw upon that Image right now as I breathe, feel and see. I am awake to life. I refute thoughts of dejection, sadness, and fatigue to experience Divine Joy. I approve, support, and confirm cheerful, lighthearted, and elated thoughts to support the Image of Perfection. I have zest and zeal to move through any event that takes place in my life. I am refreshed, restored and renewed by my thoughts of the Image of Perfection. I am rejuvenated and relieved. I seek feelings, images, and thoughts that are inspirational and fulfilling in bringing me to the full realization of Life. I draw upon that wellspring of Joy and Power to live a life that is productive and fulfilling. I am alive, filled with vitality vigor and vim. I transcend all feelings, images and thought unlike Life itself. I am important to this world. I am a vital part of the totality of life. I want to live. I now entertain feelings, images, and thoughts to give me the energy that I need for the duration of this experience. It is my nature to be alive, filled with energy. I Move quickly, easily and buoyantly. I now know that I am of value. I love Life. I have the freedom, the power, and the privilege to direct my life, and I am in charge. For this I am grateful.

Physical State: Body/Dis-ease   Ligaments
Emotional State: Soul – trust, duty
Mental State: Mind – strain, stress, burden
Spiritual State: Law – Power (undeveloped)

I take dominion and govern my feelings, images, and thoughts. I have definite results in mind. I am specific in considering the Image in which I am made. I have the essence of trust to accomplish as my duty to the Image in which I am made. I refuse to accept feelings, images, and thoughts of strain, stress and burden to express Divine Power. I accept thoughts of relaxation, self worth and freedom to live from the Image in which I am made. I am loyal, assured and accountable for my expression of Divine Power. I am dependable. It is effortless and easy to yield to the Image in which I am made as my confidence rises out of that Image to express Divine Power. I am fulfilled. Every feeling, image and thought is significant to my expression of Divine Power. I accept all feelings, images, and thoughts as guides to lead me back to the Image in which I am made. I place my faith in my feelings, images, and thoughts to lead me to live from the Image in which I am made. I remove all judgments placed on my feelings, images, and thoughts as I am now aware of the Image in which I am made as who I am. This event is my opportunity to express Divine Power and uncover the Image in which I am made. I have the knowledge, confidence and courage to express Divine Power. I dwell upon thoughts that are loyal and devoted to expressing Divine Power. I embrace thoughts that are amicable, congenial, and noble. I place full credence in my thoughts to lead me to the Image in which I am made. I accept all feelings, images, and thoughts and see the good in them. I dwell upon those that are encouraging. I lighten up on myself, nurture myself and love myself for the decision to live from the Image in which I am made. Divine Power is my strength. Divine Power is my action. I move through this and all events with a certainty and assurance. I am made free. In confidence and gratitude, I let it go.

Physical State: Body/Dis-ease   Liver
Emotional State: Soul – praise, tranquility, worship
Mental State: Mind – anger, regret, criticism
Spiritual State: Law – Love (undeveloped)

I turn my attention to that which I desire to have and I am free to acknowledge, invite and accept only that which is pleasing to me. Through Divine Love, I find peace and fulfillment. I look upon each event with interest and view each effort with enthusiasm. This unity of interest, enthusiasm and understanding develops love. In love and tranquility I turn to the Image in which I am made to restore this condition to one of acceptance. Therefore, I refuse to believe anger, regret and critical thinking supports Divine Love. I make firm in my mind thoughts of love, comfort and compliment to express Divine Love. I take great delight, honor and revere in my feelings, images, and thoughts to express from the Image in which I am made. I applaud, approve and venerate my feelings, images, and thoughts to express Divine Love. I commend myself for the reverence I now have for the Image in which I am made. I am safe, assured and successful in restoring this event to one of service, balance and honor. I compliment myself for the capacity to remain undaunted in my desire to live from the Image in which I am made. I faithfully devote myself to ruling out of my life all that is not in harmony with the Image in which I am made. I accept my feelings, images, and thoughts as the tool in guiding me to express Divine Love. I am never separated from my feelings, images, and thoughts as I am one with all parts of me. I am unified, consolidated and at one with the Image in which I am made. Therefore I embrace feelings of adoration, devotion and regard for the Image in which I am made. I am patient with myself as Divine Love flow through me. I view my feelings, images, and thoughts as necessary in fulfilling my desire to live from the Image in which I am made. I am unified with thoughts of love.

Physical State: Body/Affairs   Love
Emotional State: Soul — devotion, charity, fervor
Mental State: Mind — passion, idealism, transport
Spiritual State: Law — Love (undeveloped)

I am in love with life. I embrace my feelings, images, and thoughts about love and become devoted to bring them in union with the Image of Perfection. I especially honor myself in this experience and gratefully allow love to flow into every feeling, image, and thought about love. I hold my Image in high regard and establish a sense of devotion to that Image. I claim perfect understanding in all that I feel, imagine and say. I have the capacity to bring out the essence of passion in my desire to express Divine Love. I embrace my Ideal as the Image of Perfection and am transported to a state of mind where I dwell in loving feelings, images, and thoughts. I am wise and judicious in determining my purpose to express Divine Love. I am filled with zeal, sincerity and adhere to my desire to uncover the Image of Perfection that I am. I develop a passion for love. I experience fervor. I am attracted to feelings, images, and thoughts of love and direct my attention to developing a pattern to express love in all that I do. I am active and alive with an intense desire to develop my true nature as a Spiritual Being. I am Spiritual. I am not what I do. I accept my feelings, images, and thoughts to accomplish my special purpose to radiate Divine Love. I live in understanding and thankfulness as I see love personified in all that I do. I live to send for love, and love is returned to me. My actions are filled with love. Love frees me to enjoy the good that I deserve in Life. I accept Divine Love and see it in everything I do. My feelings, images, and thoughts are in alignment with their purpose: to bring love into my life and experience bliss. I give thanks, and it is done.

Physical State: Body/Dis-ease/Appearance   Lumps
Emotional State: Soul – inspiration, trust, transport
Mental State: Mind – frustration, boredom, hostility
Spiritual State: Law – Joy (undeveloped)

I now become aware of the Image in which I am made. All that I need is provided from the Image in which I am made. My body is now transformed into the awareness of my relationship with the Image in which I am made. I am filled with joy. I am inspired to trust the Image in which I am made and consciously move into that Image. I disavow the necessity of frustration, boredom and hostility to express Divine Joy. I assert feelings, images, and thoughts that foster, incite and agree are the foundation to express Divine Joy. I am stimulated, motivated, and encouraged by thoughts that bring excitement, interest and delight. I honor my feelings, images, and thoughts and accept the guidance I receive to express Divine Joy. I am sustained by the essence of Divine Joy. I hold my feelings, images, and thoughts in high esteem in my discernment of the Image in which I am made. My faith is reestablished and I am gentle with myself. I accept who I am and express Divine joy in all my undertakings. I am devoted to and thrive upon Divine Love. I am patient, subdued and modest in comprehending each idea to express the Image in which I am made. This event is a tool that leads me to heights of bliss, ecstasy and happiness. I love myself. I praise myself. I honor who I am. I revere my feelings, images, and thoughts as my guide to express Divine Joy and all endeavors. I am filled with enthusiasm as I express Divine Joy. My trust is in the Image in which I am made and I rely upon that part of me to restore my body to health. I perceive this world though the eyes of Joy. In complete assurance I submit to the Image in which I am made and I am free to express Divine Joy. I participate in activities that bring gaiety, delight and cheer. I call upon Divine Joy to fill my being. I assume my duty to express Divine Joy in thanksgiving and praise.

Physical State: Body/Dis-ease/Appearance   Lung
Emotional State: Soul –bliss, ecstasy, rapture
Mental State: Mind – grief, sadness, desolation
Spiritual State: Law – Life (undeveloped)

I now draw upon the Image in which I am made to express Divine Life. I breathe the breath of life and it animates my body to respond to life. I now relax. I take dominion over my feelings, images, and thoughts to experience bliss, ecstasy and rapture. Divine Joy, delight and elation are the result. I am at peace. I refuse to entertain feelings, images, and thoughts of grief, sadness and desolation as necessary to express Divine Life. I accept and entertain thoughts of comfort, happiness and encouragement to restore my body. I utilize each thought to lead me to the Image in which I am made. Life in this world is mine to live and enjoy now. My optimism becomes my faith and my belief. I accept feelings, images, and thoughts that are life-giving, life- supporting, and life-sustaining. My feelings, images, and thoughts come to honor me in my inborn desire to enlarge the Life that is within me to its fullest potential. I honor the Image in which I am made by accepting my choice to be fully alive, loving, healthy and happy. I love and approve of myself while I rejoice in expressing Divine Life. My life is made easy, prosperous and successful as I express Divine Life. I am filled with joy. I participate in life. I seize every opportunity to express Divine Life. I view my life from a different viewpoint as I embrace the Image in which I am made. I let go all feelings, images, and thoughts no longer needed to bring forward the pure essence of Life. I discover new talents, abilities and resources from within and put them to use. My thoughts enable me to live, love and meet more of Life as I live from the Image in which I am made. I rejoice in my ability to create and love as I work, play and sleep, to live from the Image in which I am made. All feelings, images, and thoughts are welcome as I move in action, feeling, and thought to receive the essence of Divine Life in this experience. I am in praise and thanksgiving for a good life.

Physical State: Body/Dis-ease /Appearance   Lupus
Emotional State: Soul – passion, bliss, rapture
Mental State: Mind – grief, sadness, frigidity
Spiritual State: Law – Life (undeveloped)

I now draw upon the Image in which I am made to express Divine Life. Every event in my life is for my highest good and I accept this event to see the good in it and experience Divine Life. I prepare my mind to experience passion, bliss and rapture. I am fervent as I am exalted into waves of Joy. I take delight in expressing Divine Life. I am eager, earnest and enthusiastic as I assess my feelings, images, and thoughts to express Divine Life. I do not accept grief, sadness and frigidity as supportive of my desire to express Divine Life. I accept, embrace and court feelings, images, and thoughts to rejoice, which brings happiness and warmth to my life. I am consoled, encouraged and comforted by the Image in which I am made. I entertain feelings, images, and thoughts of cheer, gladness and glee as necessary to experience the Image in which I am made. I exercise selectivity and use good judgment in entertaining all thoughts. I am balanced and orderly. I draw upon the Life force within me to be creative and productive. I am inspired from the Image in which I am made. I delight in knowing that I am alive, filled with vim, vigor and vitality. I love Life and Life loves me. I participate in activities that bring forth my aliveness. I cooperate with the Image in which I am made to exalt my feelings, images, and thoughts to heights of bliss. I am made aware of activities that allow for full participation in life. I embrace feelings, images, and thoughts of adoration, devotion and regard for who I am. I am patient with myself. I faithfully devote myself to ruling out of my life all feelings, images, and thoughts that are not in harmony with my desire to express Divine Life. I love, praise and applaud myself for my ability to comprehend the meaning of Life. I am warm and cordial in my assessment of my feelings, images, and thoughts to express Divine Life. I am grateful for this realization of the purpose for this condition.

Physical State: Body/Dis-ease   Lymphatic System
Emotional State: Soul – enthusiasm, fervor, devotion
Mental State: Mind – bitter, hurt, offensive
Spiritual State: Law – Joy (undeveloped)

Love holds me steady and joy fills me. From this, I give and receive love into my world. I become aware of the Image in which I am made to restore my body to its original purpose. I have reverence for the Image in which I am made. I accept, approve and welcome each opportunity to express Divine Joy. I appreciate who I am. I have high regard for my feelings, images, and thoughts and I relish, cherish and value each occasion to express Divine Joy. I open up to receive the essence of enthusiasm, fervor and devotion to live from the Image in which I am made. Delight, passion and commitment come for me to express Divine Joy. Therefore, thoughts of bitterness, hurt and offensiveness are not necessary to express Divine Joy. I embrace delightful, relieving and conciliating thoughts to dwell upon from the Image in which I am made. I celebrate, honor and cherish the possibility of expressing Divine Joy in this event. I approve, welcome and regard highly the Image in which I am made. I cooperate with life to bring about activity that enhances and expands my capacity to express Divine Joy. I am sustained, relieved and aided in my desire to live from the Image in which I am made. I appreciate knowing that all thoughts are from Ideas of Love and joy to express the essence of goodness, gentleness and ease. My trust is in the Image in which I am made. I approve of myself. I anticipate each endeavor with zest and zeal. I praise myself for the commitment to live from the Image in which I am made. I find fulfillment. I accept my feelings, images, and thoughts as the part of me that points the way for me to live from the Image in which I am made. Faithfully, I devote myself to expressing Divine Joy. I am in total agreement with my feelings, images, and thoughts as the basis for expressing Divine Joy. I accept Divine Joy in peace. I am filled with joy.

Physical State: Body/Dis-ease/Appearance   Male Problems
Emotional State: Soul – humility, virtue, generosity
Mental State: Mind – guilt, embarrassment, irritation
Spiritual State: Law – Power (undeveloped)

I now turn in thought from all appearances to know the truth about me. I turn towards the Image in which I am made to know that an endless supply of everything is waiting for me to receive all that I need. Wisdom comes with the power of truth and I now know the truth. Therefore, I turn from facts, appearances, and situations, which are always changing, and turn to the Image in which I am made. I am humble, honest and merciful in my approach to uncover the Image in which I am made. I am generous in my assessment of my feelings, images, and thoughts to express Divine Power. I refuse to believe that guilt, shame and regret are necessary to experience Divine Power. I make firm in my mind thoughts of innocence, worthiness and sanctity to experience Divine Power. I praise, honor, and elevate my Idea of the Image in which I am made. I am exonerated from judgments placed on my feelings, images, and thoughts. My feelings, images, and thoughts are my guide tools to lead me to the Image in which I am made. I respect who I am. I value this chance to express Divine Power through the Image in which I am made. I move with confidence and valor as I accept my stability in the Image in which I am made. I allow my thoughts to lead me to ideas of success, strength, and self-confidence. Divine Wisdom comes with Divine Power. I trust the Image in which I am made to guide me to thoughts of self worth, self-confidence, and a healthy self-esteem. I forgive myself. I draw upon that Image in which I am made to express Divine Power. My source is the wellspring of Divine Power within the Image in which I am made. I take dominion over my feelings, images, and thoughts and live from my true nature. I accept who I am. My acceptance depends upon my freedom to bring Divine Power into my life, and I do it now. In gratitude, I give thanks for the realization of this truth about me.

Physical State: Body/Affairs   Mastery
Emotional State: Soul – preparedness, victory, conquest
Mental State: Mind – leadership, knowledge
Spiritual State: Law – Mastery (undeveloped)

I am made in the Image of Perfection. I have all that I need to experience mastery over my feelings, images, and thoughts. I resolve all thought to accomplish my heart's desire. Wisdom comes to me. I am intelligent, knowledgeable and have the ability to govern my feelings, images, and thoughts. I speak the truth about who I am. I have the authority, power, and guidance to direct my life to accomplish my heart's desire. I allow my feelings, images, and thoughts to influence my actions to gain mastery over my life. I no longer look outside myself for direction and guidance. I am complete. I accomplish my desire to rise to that place in mind. I have the self-assurance and self-reliance to fulfill my quest to gain mastery over my feelings, images, and thoughts. I am wise in my assessment of my life and command stewardship of myself to see through the veil of illusion. I know who I am. I remind myself that I am superior to my feeling, images and thoughts to achieve my goal. I am unique. I seek wisdom from the Image of Perfection and I am provided with facts to accomplish my goal. I have been given guardianship over my life and I now realize that I have a duty to myself to fulfill my destiny to move into the state of Mastery. I am successful. I have supremacy over my feelings, images, and thoughts to know that I can attain mastery. I am effective. Prosperity, success and fulfillment are the results of my efforts to gain mastery over my feelings, images, and thoughts. I am gentle in my assessment of who I am, and I accept this experience as good and very good. In gratitude and thanksgiving, I let go and accept my gift of mastery right now.

Physical State: Body/Dis-ease/Appearance   Memory (loss)
Emotional State: Soul – unity, wholeness, mastery
Mental State: Mind – isolated, agitated, frustrated
Spiritual State: Law – Love (undeveloped)

I have the power to change anything in my life that I want to change by turning to the Image in which I am made. I now have the liberty love and power to restore my mind to recall everything I need to recall. I am nourished, sustained and fulfilled by that Image in which I am made. I have the cooperative, all embracing and loyalty of my feelings, images, and thoughts to express Divine Love. Therefore, I refute isolation, agitation, and frustration as necessary to express Divine Love. I prove to myself that as I unite my feelings, images, and thoughts to calm myself, help comes to me when I ask for it. I am obedient to the Image in which I am made. I cooperate and bring together my feelings, images, and thoughts. I find I am apt, adroit, and proficient in my efforts to live from the Image in which I am made. As I recall my purpose, my feelings, images, and thoughts are blended with ease to accomplish supremacy in expressing Divine Love. I accept, thrive upon and embrace Divine Love as it flows through me. I express Divine Love in tenderness, endearment, and sentiment. I experience the powerful, healing Presence. The activity of Divine Love flows freely through me. I am now and forever inspired with the life of the Image in which I am made. I rejoice in giving myself and my talents to all humankind. I am liberal in my view of my self-worth and capabilities. I am generous to myself. I love myself. I nurture my feelings, images, and thoughts. I align my feelings, images, and thoughts to express Divine Love. That is my true nature. I am grateful for the understanding of who I am. I take great delight in living from the Image in which I am made. I cooperate with myself. I am vigorous in my desire to express Divine Love. I am aware, alert, and awake. I live the fullness of Life in Divine Love, thanksgiving, and praise.

Physical State: Body/Dis-ease/Appearance   Menopause
Emotional State: Soul – confidence, endurance, reverence
Mental State: Mind – anxiety, fear, confusion
Spiritual State: Law – Power (undeveloped)

Right now, I am established in riches and the abundance of good. Success and prosperity meet me from every side. I open my mind to receive Divine Power and place no restrictions or limitations on my feelings, images, and thoughts to move though this event. Confidence, endurance and reverence are welcomed in this event, now that I understand that my purpose is to express Divine Power. I take dominion over my feelings, images, and thoughts and trust, in the Image in which I am made. Fortitude and regard come to me to face all events. I refuse to believe anxiety, fear and confusion are supportive of my desire to live from the Image in which I am made. I find relief. I am brave and have clarity in discerning my feelings, images, and thoughts. I am courageous, practical and have the assurance that this event is to strengthen my resolve to live from the Image in which I am made. I have the tenacity, perseverance, and security that Divine Power is my inheritance and I value, honor and respect who I am. I am in awe. I turn to the Image in which I am made and I am productive, composed and efficient in expressing Divine Power in every area of my life. I am never alone. I move with certainty and sureness. I take deliberate action in viewing my feelings, images, and thoughts. I am patient with myself. My desire to express the Divine is profitable, beneficial and successful. I am at peace. I am joy-filled and prosperous as wisdom comes to me from the Image in which I am made. I welcome new feelings, images, and thoughts to fulfill my desire to live from the Image in which I am made. I receive each thought in its fullness, sparing nothing—bringing it to express the Divine Idea of Power. I love myself and praise who I am. I am grateful for this knowledge of the Image in which I am made. I move joyfully through this experience in peace. I release myself to express Divine Power.

Physical State: Body/Dis-ease   Mind
Emotional State: Soul – discernment, sagacity, comprehension
Mental State: Mind – apprehension, fear, anxiety
Spiritual State: Law – Wisdom (undeveloped)

In this moment, I am content with the knowledge of who I am. I see Divine Wisdom in discovering who I am. I use foresight, prudence and astuteness in making all decisions about my life. I am successful in all undertakings. I move though this experience joyously and victoriously. I now embrace he Image in which I am made to express Divine Wisdom. My faculties of discernment, sagacity and comprehension are sound. I perceive in awe, the wisdom in this event and grasp the Intelligence within the Image in which I am made. Therefore, apprehension, fear and anxiety have no part in my observation of my feelings, images, and thoughts. I face the future with amazement, determined to express Divine Wisdom from the Image in which I am made. I exercise good judgment, clarity of mind and celebrate in assessing my feelings, images, and thoughts. I am wise. I allow and accept the wisdom in my feelings, images, and thoughts to guide me to my desire to live from the Image in which I am made. I court my feelings, images, and thoughts as tools to direct me to the Image in which I am made. I now know the purpose of this event and I rejoice. I remove the judgment from my feelings, images, and thoughts as I affirm, with deep conviction that these tools guide me to the Image in which I am made. I have confidence in the Image in which I am made. I move in expectancy and joy, now that I know the purpose of this event. My perception is keen. My thoughts are elevated. I praise myself for accepting this event as one that leads me to the Image in which I am made. I accept thoughts that bring me joy, laughter, and a feeling of gladness. I am content. I have the mental capacity to understand all feelings, images, and thoughts. I am at peace. I am satisfied with who I am. I accept myself. I love myself. Divine Wisdom flows through me in harmony. I discern the truth of me though this and all experiences.

Physical State: Body/Dis-ease/Appearance   Miscarriage
Emotional State: Soul – duty, belief, trust
Mental State: Mind – burdened, suspicious, doubtful
Spiritual State: Law – Power (undeveloped)

It is my desire to face every event in my life with love, adoration and joy. I view this event as one that requires me to live in the Image in which I am made. I embrace my duty, my belief and I trust the Image in which I am made. I am diligent, filled with conviction and faith that I am dependable and reliable. I am mature in assessing my feelings, images, and thoughts to express Divine Power. I am loyal as I submit to the Image in which I am made. I have the freedom, confidence, and certainty that this event is to lead me to the Image in which I am made. I declare that burden, suspicion, and doubt are unnecessary. I am at ease. I open myself as I draw upon the faith that is already within me from the Image in which I am made. I am responsible to fulfill my duty to express Divine Power. I respect who I am. I approve of myself. I love myself. I rejoice in myself. I praise myself. I am confident that I have the freedom within my feelings, images, and thoughts to express Divine Power in this event. I affirm and embrace all feelings, images, and thoughts as guides in accomplishing my purpose to live from the Image from which I am made. I bring forth the joy that is within me to express Divine Power. I am accountable to the Image in which I am made to experience Divine Power. I change my belief now that I know that I am made in the Image of Perfection. I call upon that Image as a guide through this experience. I move from thought to thought bringing into my life Divine ideas of Power. I view all thought with acuteness and discrimination. Perfect understanding comes to me and I take action to move with ease and grace to express Divine Power though the image in which I am made. Now that I know I have dominion over my feelings, images, and thoughts, I take charge and change them to create my destiny in every event. For this knowing, I am grateful.

Physical State: Body/Dis-ease   Mouth
Emotional State: Soul – transformation, unity, virtue
Mental State: Mind – irritable, fearful
Spiritual State: Law – Mastery (undeveloped)

I am enriched by my feelings, images, and thoughts as I assess them rightly. I am nourished by the Image in which I am made. I alter and replace my assessment upon my feelings, images, and thoughts to express Mastery over this event. I remain stable as I recognize my need for consistency to transform, unify and value my feelings, images, and thoughts. I reorganize my thinking to transmute former feelings, images, and thoughts to reflect Mastery in my world. Therefore I refuse to believe irritability and fear at any level of my being as necessary any longer. I maintain to be true that agreeable, honest and pure thoughts are the foundation upon which the Image in which I was made. I embrace all feelings, images, and thoughts in honor, favor and in integrity. I am whole. I have dominion of my feelings, images, and thoughts and command of myself to alter them to express Divine Mastery. I am at peace. I do not deviate from my resolve to express Divine Mastery. I unify my feelings, images, and thoughts to be in congruent with the Image in which I am made. I have the capacity; I understand the purpose of this event I have been given the government of my feelings, images, and thoughts to live from the Image in which I am made. I am victorious. I remain steadfast and unmovable to express Divine Mastery over this event. I am re-established with my feelings, images, and thoughts to express Divine Mastery. I give myself to the clear vision and understanding of this event. In my clarity of Purpose, I am stable, certain and brave. I move forward with grace and ease in radiating Divine Mastery in this event. I agree with life. I accept this event with love to live from the Image in which I am made. I confirm that I am made in the Image and Likeness of Perfection, and I am strengthened in this knowledge. I am stabilized in the power of Mastery. I give thanks and praise for the revelation of the truth about me. I take dominion over my feelings, images, and thoughts.

Physical State: Body/Dis-ease   Muscles
Emotional State: Soul – passion, zeal, duty
Mental State: Mind – resistance, rebellion, stubbornness
Spiritual State: Law – Power (undeveloped)

I now give full value to my feelings, images, and thoughts. I remain centered and calm. I am interested and enthusiastic about life. I cooperate with life and participate fully into everything I do. I call upon the Image in which I am made to heal all feelings, images, and thoughts unlike my true nature as I move through this event in peace. Experiences of passion, zeal and duty are attributes of the Image in which I am made and as such, I claim my divine heritage. I refute feelings, images, and thoughts of resistance, rebellion and stubbornness. I prove, vindicate, and conform to the Image in which I am made. I remain loyal to my purpose to experience Divine Power. I am and obedient in governing my feelings, images, and thoughts. I am free, flexible and responsive to expressing divine Power in my life and I am tenacious, adaptable and resolute in my resolve to express from the Image in which I am made. I am determined to live from the Image in which I am made; therefore, I reaffirm my intent, accepting the responsibility and become faithful in my devotion. I have the resilience, tenaciousness and persistence to express Divine Power. I am filled with vigor and verve to accomplish my desire to express Divine Power. I accept feelings, images, and thoughts of Divine Power. Divine Power flows through me. My feelings, images and my thoughts are tools to guide me back to the Image in which I am made. I accept, welcome and choose to participate in feelings, images, and thoughts of ease, certainty and complete assurance. I am brave. I am diligent in my resolve. I am unmovable in my desire to live from the Image in which I am made. I am filled with zest as I yield to the Image in which I am made. I stand firm as I assess my feelings, images, and thoughts and call them good and very good. I am filled with gratitude as Divine Power flows with ease and stabilizes my body. Divine Wisdom guides my every thought. I accept my power.

Physical State: Body/Dis-ease/Appearance   Nail biting
Emotional State: Soul – hope, grace, service
Mental State: Mind – frustration, dread, shyness
Spiritual State: Law – Love (undeveloped)

The Image in which I am made is Whole, Perfect, and Complete, and I am made from that Image. I now claim my right to express Divine Love through my feelings, images, and thoughts. Hope, grace, and service are part of the Image in which I am made, and I draw upon that Source to express Divine Love. I have the faith, confidence, and expectation to express Divine Love. I am exalted in my effort to experience Divine Love. I now refuse to believe in feelings, images, and thoughts I have judged to be frustration, dread, and shyness. I believe in thoughts that foster, assure, and encourage me in my desire to live from the Image in which I am made. I rise to that Image. It is my Source of Perfection. I remove all judgment from my feelings, images, and thoughts and move into total agreement in peace. I am encouraged, comforted, and fulfilled by the Image in which I am made. I am persuaded to support, honor, and glorify the Image in which I am made to express Divine Love. There is virtue in my feelings, images, and thoughts. I am brave and courageous in my stance to exalt the Image in which I am made. I claim my Divinity right now to live from the image in which I am made. I am in cooperation with all thought as every though is a guide for me to express Divine Love in all that I undertake. I am fulfilled. I am successful. I am inspired. I praise that which I am. I am exacting and virtuous in assessing my feelings, images, and thoughts to express Divine Love. I take pleasure in expressing Divine Love. I am undisturbed in my effort to express Divine Love. I feel confident. I grasp life with enthusiasm. I embrace my feelings, images, and thoughts with tenderness, kindness, and fondness. I have love for myself, and I face life with confidence and valor. I am loved. I am cared for. I have faith in the Image in which I am made. I am brave. I rejoice in this knowledge, and I live from the Image in which I am made. I am loved.

Physical State: Body/Dis-ease/Appearance   Nausea
Emotional State: Soul – endurance, awe, reverence
Mental State: Mind – rejection, fear, desolation
Spiritual State: Law – Power (undeveloped)

I am never alone. I now turn to the Image in which I am made to express endurance, awe and reverence. I have the stamina, wonder and bravery to move through this event in peace to express Divine Power. Therefore, I declare that there are no such things as rejection, fear, and desolation. I declare firmly that only feelings, images, and thoughts of acceptance, bravery, and joy have place in my world. I reestablish my life to express Divine Power through this event. I am encouraged, confident, and assured that Divine Power is my heritage as made in the Image of Perfection. I approve of myself as I am brave, daring, and persistent in my effort to live from the Image in which I am made. I am inspired. I respect the magnificence of the Image in which I am made and feel secure in allowing my feelings, images, and thoughts to guide me in all events. Divine Power flows freely and effortless through me. I am valiant, encouraged to continue my resolve to live from the Image in which I am made. I am unified in feelings, images, and thoughts and accept all as good and very good. I now understand the purpose of my feelings, images, and thoughts as my guideposts to lead me to the Image in which I am made. I move through this event joyously and victoriously. I am now established in mind to express Divine Power. I accept this event as one that leads me to the Image in which I am made. I cooperate by changing my behavior to accommodate my purpose. Divine Power provides me with boldness, happiness, and tenacity to express the Image in which I am made. I am relentless in my desire to express Divine Power. I love myself. I praise myself. I hold myself in high esteem to express Divine Power. I now rise to live from the Image in which I am made. Divine Power's overflowing stream of plenty meets my every requirement. I give thanks as I dwell within the Image in which I am made. I embrace my power.

Physical State: Body/Dis-ease   Neck
Emotional State: Soul – endurance, transmutation
Mental State: Mind – suppression, stubbornness, rejection
Spiritual State: Law – Power (undeveloped)

I stand in awe of the Image in which I am made. I unleash my feelings, images, and thoughts to change this event to express Divine Power. I am flexible, adaptable, and yielding in my recognition of the Image in which I am made. I have the stamina and the capacity to move into the Image in which I am made. I approve of and welcome the change to live in the image in which I am made. I exalt my feelings, images, and thoughts to express Divine Power. I abstain from indulging in thoughts of suppression, stubbornness, and rejection. I confirm thoughts and expressions that are pliable and acceptable as my way to experience Divine Power. I am persistent in my desire to live from the Image in which I am made. I am receptive to change. I am dutiful and assertive in expressing my desire to live from the Image in which I am made. I dwell upon thoughts of approval and commit right now to expressing Divine Power though this experience. I am at peace. I say yes to life. I participate in life, and I experience the change in my feelings, images, and thoughts. I have supremacy over my feelings, images, and thoughts and exert my dominion right now. I am resilient. I alter my feelings, images, and thoughts to express Divine Power. I am at peace with myself. I praise myself. I love myself. I receive Divine Power, which gives me a new perspective of who I am. I approve of the change that I am making to live from the Image in which I am made. I raise my thoughts to incorporate the essence of Divine Power. My feelings, images, and thoughts incite me to action; my thoughts direct my action to bring Divine Joy into my world of affairs. Thoughts come to me to lead me to the Image in which I am made; therefore, they cannot be beyond my ability to express. I bring order to my life through the knowledge of the Image in which I am made. I am still as Divine Power flows through me. With confidence in my word, I court Divine Power.

Physical State: Body/Dis-ease   Nerves
Emotional State: Soul – equanimity, tranquility, patience
Mental State: Mind – apprehensive, irritable, restive
Spiritual State: Law – Peace (undeveloped)

I exist in limitless opportunities that are forever seeking expression through me. I call upon the Image in which I am made to restore Divine Peace to rise to Its Image. I open my eyes and mind to present possibilities and discover Divine Peace. I experience success in all my undertakings. Divine Peace enables me to use the power I already possess and I am now peaceful. It is my nature to express Divine Peace with which I have been uniquely endowed. I am composed, reposed and tolerant with my feelings, images, and thoughts. I refuse to entertain feelings, images, and thoughts of apprehensiveness, irritability and restive to express Divine Peace. I accept and embrace feelings, images, and thoughts that are of confidence, delight and soothing. I draw upon order, accord, and unity as I trust the Image in which I am made. I have the balance, consistency, and symmetry needed to move into the Image in which I am made. I now understand the assistance that is given to me to express Divine Peace. I am poised. I have the stability. I unify my feelings, images, and thoughts to align with my purpose to express Divine Peace. I am tranquil, still, and calm. I am bold in my effort to express from the Image in which I am made. I am serene. I am steady. I am constant. I am in agreement with the Image in which I am made I tell myself the truth about who I am and accept that which flows through me. Divine Peace comforts me. I am sustained, healed, and prospered. Divine peace overflows my entire being. I am filled with enthusiasm and joy as I move with ease to live from the Image in which I am made. I am flooded with Divine Peace. I am calm and quiet in my assessment of my feelings, images, and thoughts. I am competent in discerning my feelings, images, and thoughts. I call the experience good and very good. I rejoice in the knowledge of the Image in which I am made. I rest in sweet repose.

Physical State: Body/Dis-ease/Appearance   Nodules
Emotional State: Soul – discernment, zeal, fervor
Mental State: Mind – discouragement, animosity
Spiritual State: Law - Power (undeveloped)

I now rise higher to experience the splendor and joy of Divine Power. I am eager to live from the Image in which I am made and my feelings, images, and thoughts foster my effort. I am delighted to express divine Power and move with vigor and vitality to express from the Image in which I am made. My desire to understand my feelings, images, and thoughts is increased. I am brave and courageous and move with valor through all feelings, images, and thoughts. I use good judgment in assessing my feelings, images, and thoughts and relish the passion that I feel to express Divine Power. I refuse to believe discouragement and animosity as necessary to express Divine Power. I make firm in my mind that feelings, images, and thoughts are to amplify my desire to live from the Image in which I am made. Congeniality, kindness, and harmony now support me in my desire to live from the Image in which I am made. I experience Divine Power as I contemplate each feeling, image, and thought. I am at peace. Divine Power flows through me to live from the Image in which I am made. I cultivate my ability to receive Divine Power. I accept this event to express Divine Power. I am wise in making a decision to bring forth the Image in which I am made. Divine Power animates me, and I am free. I govern my feelings, images, and thoughts to harmonize with the Image in which I am made. I am at peace. I feel potent, strong, and powerful as I move thought this appearance. I am filled with vigor, zest, and fervor as I live from the Image in which I am made. I am determined to express Divine Power in all my activities. I am not bound by the past, nor confounded by the future. There is only the joyous, dynamic, continuous today that I can live from the Image in which I am made. I am grateful for this opportunity to express Divine Power, and I am free. In confidence, boldness, and trust, I embrace Divine Power.

Physical State: Body/Affairs   Non-Interference
Emotional State: Soul – help, assistance, freedom
Mental State: Mind – meddling, imposing, delayed
Spiritual State: Law – Life (undeveloped)

I mind my own business. My business is to bring order and harmony into my feelings, images, and thoughts. I no longer feel that I must save the world. My world is the only world in which I have government, leadership, and authority. I allow all others the freedom to take dominion over their feelings, images, and thoughts. I respect all others as made in the Image of Perfection. I have the help I need to live in peace. I draw upon the Image of Perfection to assist and guide me in all decisions about my life. I refuse to accept thoughts of meddling, intrusion, and delays. I accept only thoughts that initiate and promote Divine Life. I free myself from placing judgments upon my feelings, images, and thoughts and accept them as tools to express the highest quality of life. I am at peace. I conduct my life in a manner to allow others the freedom to express their talents, gifts, and abilities. I mind my own business. I am alive and filled with the essence and vitality of life. I love, bless, and release all others as I turn to love to express more of Life. I am the governor of my feelings, images, and thoughts. I become clear on my purpose. I am the Source of my life. Life expresses Itself through me, and I am at peace. I face each experience with joy and gladness of heart as I refrain from interfering in others' affairs. I now know that I can never be separated from my feelings, images, and thoughts. I unify with Life. I use this experience to bring forth the essence of Life. I respect my feelings, images, and thoughts. I move forward with certainty and positive results. I give thanks for this experience as I remember who I am.

Physical State: Body/Dis-ease   Nose
Emotional State: Soul – duty, exaltation
Mental State: Mind – hostility, defiance, deception
Spiritual State: Law – Love (undeveloped)

I know that everything in my experience is working together to bring me to live from the Image in which I am made. I am thoughtful in displaying loving actions toward my feelings, images, and thoughts. I love myself and accept my feelings, images, and thoughts as my guide to live from the Image in which I am made. I am at peace. I establish a close relationship with the Image in which I am made. I have dominion over my feelings, images, and thoughts. I am loyal, patient, and kind to myself. I am gentle as I turn to the Image in which I am made to tell myself the truth. It is my duty to praise my feelings, images, and thoughts to reflect the Image in which I am made. I am faithful and conscientious. I refute feelings, images, and thoughts of hostility, defiance, and deceptiveness as I accept peaceful, obedient, and yielding feelings, images, and thoughts. I am trustworthy, truthful, and patient with myself. My feelings, images, and thoughts are my guide to live from the image in which I am made. I am worthy of love. I am filled with acceptance and cheer as I express Divine Love. Divine Love heals all. I resign myself to express Divine Love in all my activities. I am willing to change my feelings, images, and thoughts to express Divine Love. I indulge in thought of gentleness and remain steadfast and consistent with my true nature. I project a charitable, hospitable, and friendly atmosphere wherever I go as this is my true nature. My feelings are generated by my thoughts and my thoughts right now are filled with trust, conviction and devotion to the Image in which I am made. I court feelings, images, and thoughts of love. I am affectionate and patient. I love myself just as I am, as I am made in the Image of Perfection. I accept myself and rejoice in the Image in which I am made as I express Divine Love. I give thanks for this opportunity to increase the quality of my life in absolute faith and love.

Physical State: Body/Dis-ease/Appearance   Numbness
Emotional State: Soul – hope, faith, belief
Mental State: Mind – inertia, despair, grief
Spiritual State: Law – Joy (undeveloped)

I seize the good this day holds. I rise above the temptation to look back with longing at earlier days in my life, or to dream of exciting eras in far off times. This day adds to my knowledge of who I am. This day, I give love to the Image in which I am made for the right attitude toward this event. I value love, and I am appreciative of my feelings, images, and thoughts. I turn to the Image in which I am made, establish a belief in that Image, and Joy now floods my life. I am now conscious of my awareness of the Image in which I am made. Hope, faith, and belief are parts of that Image, and I now rise in confidence to be active in bringing it forth. I have the assurance, trust, and conviction that I have the capacity to live from the Image in which I am made. I am now conscious of who I am. I refute feelings, images, and thoughts of inertia, despair, and grief. I accept activity, delightful experiences, and courageous feelings, images, and thoughts to move through this experience. I express aliveness, vitality and certainty in expressing Divine Joy. I am vigorous, energetic, and sensitive to my feelings, images, and thoughts. I have the awareness of expressing Divine Joy in this event. I have the belief, conviction, and perception of the Image in which I am made. I am filled with rapture. I am cheerful. My heart is filled with the gladness of the Image in which I am made. Happiness exudes from me. I draw upon the wellspring of Life to express Divine Joy. I regard all feelings, images, and thoughts in a calm and quiet manner. I am gentle with myself. There is no belief in inactivity. Activity is Life. Activity must express through everything. I tell myself the truth. I am quiet and calm in my assessment of my feelings, images, and thoughts. I am at peace. I am at rest. I am relaxed. Divine Joy fills my being. I am competent in discerning all feelings, images, and thoughts to live from the image in which I am made.

Physical State: Body/Dis-ease/Appearance   Obesity
Emotional State: Soul – humility, worship, reverence
Mental State: Mind – shame, deception, criticism
Spiritual State: Law – Love (undeveloped)

I begin this day in praise for who I am. I am made in the Image of Perfection, therefore, perfect. I am not what I do. I am not what I feel. I am not what I think. I am made in the Image and likeness of perfection. I use my feelings to direct the life force in my body to express the attributes of who I am. I use my mind to guide me through earthly experiences. Therefore, I recognize Divine Love now flowing through me to heal all feelings, images, and thoughts that prevent me from expressing Divine Love. I praise my body, mind, and soul in all expressions of the Image in which I am made. Humility, worship, and reverence are now made part of my expression of Divine Love. I elevate, exalt, and revere the Image in which I am made. My feelings, images, and thoughts of shame, deception, and criticism are no longer necessary. I embrace, court, and encourage honor, honesty, and approval of my feelings, images, and thoughts. I respect, support, and value the Image in which I am made. I make firm in my mind feelings, images, and thoughts of honor, honesty and praise. I am trustworthy. I commend myself for who I am. I tell myself the truth and appreciate my worth. I am admirable, virtuous, and loyal to the Image in which I am made. I am important to myself and this world. I promote feelings, images, and thoughts of loyalty, virtue, and merit to live from the Image in which I am made. I cannot deviate from my true nature to express Divine Love. I embrace life in total devotion for the purpose of unfolding my greatest potential to live from the Image in which I am made. My values are true, sound, and essential to living from the Image in which I am made. My desire is to embrace life in kindness, tenderness, and gentleness. I am gentle with myself. My actions are now conformed to live from the Image in which I am made. In gratitude and thanksgiving, I am renewed in my feelings, images, and thoughts.

Physical State: Body/Dis-ease/Appearance   Osteoporosis
Emotional State: Soul — faith, reverence, endurance
Mental State: Mind — weakness, fear, consternation
Spiritual State: Law — Power (undeveloped)

The Image in which I am made impels me to move in directions to express my innate ability to express Divine Power. I move forward with confidence in my ability to express Divine Power. I welcome the opportunity to express fully, completely, and joyfully. Divine Power protects, guides, and directs me. In the Image in which I am made is that authority that impels me to move in directions for my highest good. It is that sustaining power that allows me the freedom of movement. I reach out to receive my good. My mind is alert. I am now lifted in faith, reverence and endurance to live from the Image in which I am made. I trust, regard, and have the stamina to express Divine Power. My thoughts of weakness, fear, and consternation are of no use to me any longer. I embrace feelings, images, and thoughts that are strong, brave, and confident in the Image in which I am made. I am vigorous, hardy, and steady. I am brave, safe, and secure. My thinking is solid and sound. I stand firm in my desire to live from the Image in which I am made. I remain undaunted in my efforts. I have the confidence and assurance that this event is to express Divine Power. I turn to the Image in which I am made in praise and devotion. I have the courage to live from the Image in which I am made. I am calm. I am devoted to expressing Divine Power. I now claim Divine Power to flow through me and demonstrate my true nature. My purpose is in alignment with my feelings, images, and thoughts to express Divine Power. My life is restructured to live from the Image in which I am made. I am grateful. I am at peace. I am restored. Divine Power now flows through me in peace. I choose my position right now. I am now free to express my highest ability to live from the Image in which I am made. I am secure in the knowledge of who I am. I appreciate me and my accomplishments. I now accept these words to be the truth about me as I embrace Divine Power.

Physical State: Body/Dis-ease   Ovaries
Emotional State: Soul – reverence, devotion
Mental State: Mind – abuse, disdain, scorn
Spiritual State: Law – Love (undeveloped)

I now use the liberty, love, and power within me to heal my body of this dis-ease. I free my feelings, images, and thoughts to align with my purpose to express Divine Love. Now that I understand the purpose of this event, I change the appearance by changing my feelings, images, and thoughts. I have reverence and devotion for the Image in which I am made. I turn to that Image as I dedicate myself to expressing Divine Love. I have regard, appreciation, and affection for my feelings, images, and thoughts, which are my guides to express Divine Love. I refuse to believe feelings, images, and thoughts of abuse, disdain, and scorn. I make firm in my mind and embrace caring, favor, and accepting thoughts to express Divine Love. I hold myself in high regard and esteem. I appreciate myself. I approve of myself. I honor, respect, and admire the Image in which I am made. I compliment, praise, and acclaim my feelings, images and thoughts. I seek to fulfill my desire to express Divine Love. Divine Love and power flow through me. I am honest with myself and gentle in assessing my feelings, images, and thoughts. My acceptance of my feelings, images, and thoughts allows me to surrender to the flow of Divine Love. Humility and peace come with all feelings. I have the capacity within the Image in which I am made to express Divine Love in my world. I am victorious in my efforts. I consciously participate in activities that bring out Divine Love in my life. The desire to express Divine Love is a living flame within me. My desires come from the Image in which I am made, persistently moving me forward to the great purpose of my life. I make peace with my feelings, images, and thoughts. Divine Love stimulates me to take action. I allow Divine Love to flow through me right now. I dwell upon thoughts of productivity and draw from the Image in which I am made. My mind is open to receive Divine Love, and I am fulfilled. I am grateful.

Physical State: Body/Dis-ease/Appearance   Pain
Emotional State: Soul – rapture, serenity, patience
Mental State: Mind – torment, worry, irritation
Spiritual State: Law – Peace (undeveloped)

I call upon the Image in which I am made to move through this experience. Although I have misunderstood my union with all Life, I rely upon that Image to bring forth Divine Peace. I open up to receive. I am optimistic about life. I am calm. I become patient with my feelings, images, and thoughts to express Divine Peace. I move with certainty to receive the essence of rapture, serenity, and patience. Divine Joy and calmness flow through me. I am at rest. I feel relieved. I am at ease. I refuse to accept torment, worry, and irritation. I take great delight, comfort, and a calm endurance in the knowledge of the Image in which I am made. I have the consolation, encouragement, and assurance to experience Divine Peace. I am at ease. I relax as I am soothed by bliss that flows from the Image in which I am made. I am tranquil. I trust my feelings, images, and thoughts to guide me through this event. I feel secure. I find great pleasure in knowing that I am made in the Image and likeness of Perfection. I remain tireless and diligent in my efforts to express Divine Peace. I place my confidence in the Image in which I am made. I am governed by that Image. I withstand this and all events without bending. I embrace feelings of expectation and probability. My feelings, images, and thoughts guide me to the Image in which I am made. I am encouraged. I relax and accept that I am capable of experiencing Divine Peace. My feelings are renewed. I am free from mistaken feelings, images, and thoughts, and I feel at ease in my assessment. I accept all feelings as the Divine urge to express from the Image in which I am made. All feelings are serviceable, beneficial, and wholesome – necessary to express life from the Image in which I am made. All feelings are salutary, competent, and genuine in their nature to demonstrate Divine Peace through me. For this, I am grateful.

Physical State: Body/Dis-ease/Appearance   Paralysis
Emotional State: Soul – enthusiasm, passion, transport
Mental State: Mind – apathy, escape, resistance
Spiritual State: Law – Life (undeveloped)

I awaken to the Image in which I am made. I participate in life. My faith is restored. I am motivated to take right action as I rise for new experiences to come to me. The Image in which I am made nurtures, comforts, and consoles me to realize only good. I am the image of love, and Divine Love surrounds me. I now permit my inward vision to penetrate every apparent obstruction, every attempt to hide the Image in which I am made. I withdraw the veil of ignorant misuse of my feelings, images, and thoughts. Reality is revealed to me. Reality does not change. I now face life with confidence, filled with Divine Joy and Peace to move through this event. The very essence of enthusiasm, passion, and transport now moves freely through me. I open up to receive. I am eager, filled with fervor and ecstasy as I rise to the Image in which I am made. I refute feelings, images, and thoughts of apathy to experience Divine Life. I support, endorse, and encourage my conscious involvement in my life. I am filled with zest, energy, and verve to express Divine Life. I am animated, vigorous, and filled with vitality. I take a new interest in and respond to Divine Life. I have strength. I anticipate new and enthusiastic ways of experiencing the Image in which I am made. I am in agreement with all life experiences and embrace each experience with gladness and thanksgiving. Divine Joy and peace are increasingly made real in this event. Everything I do prospers. Life is Eternal, and I reflect this Life from the Image in which I am made. I embrace Life. Eternal Life is mine right now, and I claim freedom to express it in its fullness. I am gentle with my feelings, images, and thoughts as they guide me through this event to greater involvement in my life. I take charge of my life. I have the dominion to govern my feelings, images, and thoughts, and I take dominion right now. I give thanks for the understanding of this event.

Physical State: Body/Dis-ease/Appearance   Parkinson's Disease
Emotional State: Soul – mastery, dominion, grace
Mental State: Mind – fear, impatience, awkwardness
Spiritual State: Law – Power (undeveloped)

I am free of any and all limited belief in the process of life. I move into the true belief that life is Eternal in the Image in which I am made. As joy is part of that Image, I am enthusiastic in participating in life experiences. I am at peace. I minister to all feelings, images, and thoughts with favor. I am generous in my assessment to receive and give Divine Power. I take government over my world to master, govern, and skillfully shape my life to the Image in which I am made. I deny fear, incompetence, and awkwardness as necessary to express Divine Power. I affirm bravery, efficiency, and effortlessness as my tools to express Divine Power. I am free to govern, command, and take authority over my feelings, images, and thoughts. I do so now. I am loving, kind, and gentle in assessing my feelings, images, and thoughts as they are my guides. I trust the Image in which I am made and attain the efficiency, adroitness, and sanctity to move though this event. I am sensible and direct in my approach. I tell myself the truth. I am brave, strong, and dexterous. I am filled with vim, vigor, and vitality. I take great pleasure in feelings, images, and thoughts of greatness, importance, and high spirit. I rely upon courage, honor, and regard from the Image in which I am made. I give in to feelings, images, and thoughts of union, completion, and resolution. I surrender to the Image in which I am made in peace. I move with a lightness of heart and an undaunted spirit, and I claim Divine Power. I am now motivated and inspired to lift all feelings, images, and thoughts to the Image in which I am made. My thoughts flow to me to express Divine Power from the Image in which I am made. I call upon Divine Power as I move through this experience. I am restored, revitalized, and capable of expressing Divine Power. I honor my power.

Physical State: Body/Affairs   Patience
Emotional State: Soul – persistence, fortitude
Mental State: Mind – resistance, irritation
Spiritual State: Law – Peace (undeveloped)

I now make wise use of my inner gift of patience and let go of all feelings, images, and thoughts of impatience. I am calm, forgiving, and loving in all my actions. I judge not. I am set free from all that is unlike love. Love reigns in my heart and purifies my thinking about myself. Patience allows me to accept all ideas that flow through me to encourage peaceful action. I now take dominion over my feelings, images, and thoughts to declare the truth in my world of affairs. My life is good. My life is part of all Life, and as I accept Life, I am at peace. I am relentless in my pursuits to experience life in peace. I have the endurance, courage, and strength of mind to govern my feelings, images, and thoughts about any event in my life. I refuse to believe thoughts of resistance and irritation as necessary to express Divine Peace. I make firm in my mind that I have resolved to express Divine Peace, and this experience is to inspire and remind me of who I am. I have the tenacity, valor, and bravery to move through every event in peace. I am bold in my assertion of this truth. I accept that I am made in the Image of Perfection and draw upon this image right now to restore my feelings, images, and thoughts to the purpose of peace. I take delight in this experience to develop Divine Peace. I am at ease. I claim armistice, suspension, and truce to all thoughts contrary to my Divine Purpose to express the Image in which I am made. I now align my thoughts and actions to support that Image. I am at peace. I rest in sweet repose. I feel secure, thinking only thoughts of freedom to experience Divine Peace. I give thanks for peace of mind and accept it as so.

Physical State: Body/Affairs   Peace
Emotional State: Soul – harmony, tranquility, serenity
Mental State: Mind – conflict, agitation, chaos
Spiritual State: Law – Divine Peace (undeveloped)

I am now guided into pathways of peace. I am filled with confidence as joy fills my being. I move with sureness of speech and action. I am in agreement with my feelings, images, and thoughts; harmony is my natural state. I rest in sweet repose. I center my attention upon Divine Peace. I open my thoughts to the influx of Divine Intelligence and my heart to the warmth of Divine Peace. I turn my attention from appearances and direct it to the Image in which I am made. I know the serenity that results in an all-pervading peace in my world. I refute all thoughts of conflict, agitation, and chaos as necessary to express Divine Peace. I approve, accept, and confirm thoughts of concord, composure, and order. I am at peace with Life. I accept Its fullness, knowing that I have the courage to fulfill Its every need. My feelings, images, and thoughts are my tools to experience Divine Peace. My mind is filled with thoughts of contentment, and I am in concordance with these thoughts. I feel secure. I am calm. I am tranquil in thoughts and action. My mind is at peace. I trust in the Image of Perfection and experience the vitality and harmony of Divine Peace. I align my feelings, images, and thoughts to express Divine Peace. I let go, relax. I feel content. I am untroubled, unruffled, and reposeful. I am serene and cheerful as Divine Peace flow through my world. I am quiet. I am free to express unity in my world. I am composed, self possessed, and undisturbed. I am gentle with my feelings, images, and thoughts as I move through this event. I am serene. I give thanks for the restoration of Divine Peace in my world and accept that it is already done.

Physical State: Body/Dis-ease   Pelvis
Emotional State: Soul – harmony, accord, unity
Mental State: Mind – conflict, strife, deceitfulness
Spiritual State: Law – Peace (undeveloped)

I do all that I need to do whenever the time is right. I know what to do and when to go about doing it. I rest in sweet repose, knowing all is well. I am free to express Divine Peace in every area of my life. I free my feelings, images, and thoughts from all ideas unlike the Image in which I am made. I am consistent in my actions and concur with my feelings, images, and thoughts to express Divine Peace. I move forward in forthrightness, truthfulness, and unanimity in assessing my feelings, images, and thoughts. I am fulfilled. I succeed. I change my position to express Divine Peace. My purpose in this event is to express the Image in which I am made. Harmony, accord, and unity are my tools. I use them wisely. I refuse feelings, images, and thoughts of conflict, strife, and deceitfulness as a way to express Divine Peace. I accept agreement, calmness, and honesty to express Divine Peace. I am in unison with my purpose. I harbor no unkind thought. I dwell on no unkind deed. I elevate my feelings, images, and thoughts through praise for myself and all others. My life and experiences now have greater meaning for me. Appearances come to me to guide me to my true nature to live from the Image in which I am made. I participate in my life. I am filled with joy and expectation of new and genuine ideas to unfold my greatest potential. I take action to achieve my purpose to express Divine Peace. I live from the Image in which I am made. I accept my Divine Right to express Divine Peace. I move with certainty and sureness. I take deliberate action in moving into the Image in which I am made. My affairs are in divine order. I express supreme confidence in my ability to live from the Image in which I am made. I am patient with myself. I am generous with my feelings, images, and thoughts. I affirm my complete agreement with myself to live from the Image in which I am made. I am at peace. Divine Peace floods my being. In gratitude, with calm, complete conviction, I accept these words as Truth for my life.

Physical State: Body/Dis-ease/Appearance   Phlebitis
Emotional State: Soul – enlightenment, order, faith
Mental State: Mind – confusion, doubt, distrust
Spiritual State: Law – Wisdom (undeveloped)

I am conscious that I know what to do, and I am impelled to act intelligently upon every right impression. I am reliable in my understanding of how to serve the Image in which I am made, and I surrender myself completely to it. I have complete faith and self-confidence in my ability to express Divine Wisdom. I am informed as I direct my faith to the Image in which I am made. I now live my life with great ease and comfort and move from thought to feeling effortlessly. I direct my thoughts in such a manner that I mentally embody those experiences that I desire in my progress toward my goals. Discomforts reflect my inner thoughts. I now change the appearance of this discomfort by turning to the Image in which I am made. I clear my mind of confusion, doubt, and distrust as I embrace, honor, and court clarity, faith, and trust. I am enlightened. My world is now in order. My thoughts now flow from the Image in which I am made. I am at peace. I cannot be disturbed by outer events as I call upon the Image in which I am made. I have the confidence, certainty, and perception of the Image in which I am made. I express the wholeness of life in this experience, and I am in perfect agreement with my feelings, images, and thoughts. I am determined to establish my trust in the Image in which I am made. I resolve to clarify my feelings, images, and thoughts to express Divine Wisdom. I make the decision to put all feelings, images, and thoughts in order to express Divine Wisdom. I accept all experiences, as each experience leads me to live from the Image in which I am made. I have confidence, trust, and reliance upon myself to live from the Image in which I am made. Divine Wisdom brings ideas of freedom and joy. My feelings, images, and thoughts come to me to lead me to the Image in which I am made. I am grateful for the realization of this truth.

Physical State: Body/Dis-ease/Appearance   Pink Eye
Emotional State: Soul – inspiration, discrimination, clarity
Mental State: Mind – frustration, hostility, anger
Spiritual State: Law – Peace (undeveloped)

The Image in which I am made is my highest Intelligence. My feelings, images, and thoughts are my heritage to live from the Image in which I am made. I recognize them as my safe guard, my stepping stone into the Image in which I am made. Inspiration, discernment, and clarity are my tools to live from the Image in which I am made. I become responsible for my feelings, images, and thoughts and bring lucidity into my actions. I distinguish that which is right and best for me. I love myself. I praise myself. I adore who I am. I refute feelings, images, and thoughts of frustration, hostility, and anger to express Divine Peace. I accept, agree, and embody refined, loving, and friendly thoughts to express Divine Peace. I develop my vision to support, regard and assist me in expressing Divine Peace. I open my eyes to see the truth in this event. I am grateful for the Image in which I am made. I trust the Image in which I am made to balance my world. I see clearly and with wisdom. Success is mine as I work toward living from the Image in which I am made. I appreciate myself. I love myself. My feelings, images, and thoughts foster, encourage and assist me in my effort to live from the Image in which I am made. I approve of myself. I give royally, freely, and cheerfully to my feelings, images, and thoughts. I receive Divine Peace. I am at rest. My feelings, images, and thoughts are elevated to receive Divine Peace. I am filled with cheer. I am tranquil. I am still. I rest in sweet repose. I experience success in all that I undertake. I am calm and quiet in my evaluation of my feelings, images, and thoughts. I am gentle with myself. I stand firm upon my belief of who I am, and I see clearly. I change my perception of my feelings, images, and thoughts and rise to that Image. I am stimulated, encouraged and sagacious. I rejoice in the knowledge of who I am.

Physical State: Body/Dis-ease/Appearance   Pneumonia
Emotional State: Soul – hope, faith, determination
Mental State: Mind – deep hurts, desperation, tiredness
Spiritual State: Law – Life (undeveloped)

I am alive and filled with the essence of Life. I seize life fully and live from the Image in which I am made. I refrain from placing judgments upon my feelings, images, and thoughts and accept them as tools to express life. I am at peace. I become clear on my purpose in Life as I live from the Image in which I am made. Life expresses itself through me, and I seize each opportunity with willingness to experience the Image in which I am made. I draw upon the essence and vitality of the Image in which I am made. I face each experience with joy and gladness of heart as I welcome the experience of hope, faith, and trust. I have the confidence, belief, and determination to live from the Image in which I am made. I do not accept feelings, images, and thoughts of deep hurt, desperation, and tiredness. I change the appearance right now, to accept, embrace, and court feelings that are pleasurable, calm, and invigorated. I take great delight, consolation, and comfort in knowing that I am made in the Image and likeness of Perfection. I find relief and ease. I am content as I rely upon the Image in which I am made to support me in this event. I am bold, determined, and satisfied that my feelings, images, and thoughts are my guides. I am filled with joy. I anticipate a complete restoration of this event to express Divine Life. I am enlivened. I trust who I am. I have the capabilities to express Divine Life. I take a renewed interest in life, as I awaken to the Image in which I am made. I order my life to find joy in living. I look forward with great expectation to expressing Divine Life. I am honorable in my intent to uncover the essence of Life through my feelings, images, and thoughts. I participate in thoughts that are certain and reliable. I am enough. I have enough. I uncover the Image in which I am made and live from that Image. I express life through my feelings, images, and thoughts. I embrace all of me and allow this appearance to dissipate. I give thanks and praise that my health is restored.

Physical State: Body/Affairs   Power
Emotional State: Soul —authority, dominion, faculty
Mental State: Mind — weakness, impotence, frailty
Spiritual State: Law — Power (undeveloped)

I am aware of the pulse of Life moving through my feelings, images, and thoughts. I am made in the Image of Perfection, complete and fulfilled, here and now. I believe in the efficacy of my feelings, images, and thoughts through my faith. I have the capacity and power of dominion over my life. I have the authority, dominion, and faculty to claim that power right now. I am endowed with Divine Power, and I call upon my innate ability to exert that power right now. I refuse thoughts of weakness, impotence, and frailty as I accept thoughts of strength—the capacity to move through this experience in joy. I am sturdy, robust, and vigorous. I am healthy, filled with vim and vitality. I find strength and comfort in determining what is for my highest good. I claim my power to overcome all appearances of powerlessness, weakness, and incompetence. I am effective. I am courageous in all my actions as I draw upon the Image of Perfection. I claim my power to bring change into my life under the guidance of my feelings, images, and thoughts. I take leadership over my life. I am empowered. I draw upon Divine Power to fill my mind with clear directions. I have the potential to rise above my feelings, images, and thoughts. I draw upon my inner strength to accomplish all that is required of me. I determine what is important in my Life and refuse to accept anything I do not desire to experience. I accept my responsibility to live a rich and fulfilled life. I am unique. I have the fortitude to cultivate my potential. I begin this moment to discover Divine Power, which enables me to accomplish my purpose. I am grateful for this realization as I seize my power.

Physical State: Body/Affairs   Prejudice
Emotional State: Soul – equality, tolerance
Mental State: Mind – contamination, hurt, injustice
Spiritual State: Law – Peace (undeveloped)

I now let love live through me and bring forward that which is kind, compassionate and noble. In these qualities, I find fulfillment. I become enthusiastic about living and aware of the opportunity to enjoy this life. I no longer judge by appearances or facts. I look for and see justice, fairness, and uniformity in all my feelings, images, and thoughts. I am tolerant of myself. I do not accept thoughts of contamination, hurt, or injustice. I accept, embrace, and court feelings, images, and thoughts of purity, pleasure, and fairness to move through this event. I delight in uncovering the Image in which I am made; therefore, I seek feelings of ecstasy, joy, and serenity. I see the good in all situations and conditions. I am relieved. My world is restored to Divine Peace. I greet the appearance of prejudice in my world of affairs as unreal; it has no substance or life. I welcome all appearances to guide me to my true nature. I am not against anything. My true nature is of love and joy. My feelings, images, and thoughts allow me to be open to compatibility and courtesy and send out Divine Qualities of the Image of Perfection. I am unlimited in my ability to govern my feelings, images, and thoughts to express Divine Peace. I keep my promise to myself to express Divine Peace. I regard, admire, and show fondness for myself. I accept, welcome, and dwell upon thoughts that influence friendship, fairness, and justice. Light flows through my thoughts for acceptance. I judge according to Divine Love and Divine Peace. I am in agreement with my feelings, images, and thoughts as I embrace Divine Peace.

Physical State: Body/Dis-ease   Prostate
Emotional State: Soul – accord, unity, reverence
Mental State: Mind – confusion, anger, conflict
Spiritual State: Law – Love (undeveloped)

Love is the quality that grows through giving. I now make a habit of giving love to develop the Image in which I am made to express Divine Love. I choose the greater potential. The challenge of the unknown spurs me on to face that which lies ahead. I trust my feelings, images, and thoughts to move me through this experience. I move into unexplored areas of thought and activity with great courage. I now embrace agreement, unity, and reverence as my tools to express Divine Love. I desire to be loved; therefore, I must first learn how to love. I give love to my feelings, images, and thoughts. I am not what I feel; I am not what I think; and I am not what I do. I am made in the Image and likeness of Perfection, and I claim my perfection now. Love is all forgiving, and I forgive myself for judgments placed on my feelings, images, and thoughts. I refuse to believe or participate in confusion, anger, and conflict any longer. I accept, believe in, and embrace orderliness, bravery, and support. Enlightenment comes to me. I harmonize, reconcile, and approve of my feelings, images, and thoughts to live from the Image in which I am made. I welcome all feelings, images, and thoughts and call them good and very good. I regard my feelings highly and have a natural affinity with them. I have confidence and assurance in my ability to express Divine Love. I feel secure. I take delight in this new knowledge of the Image in which I am made. I hold deep and abiding respect for the Image in which I am made. I now unify my feelings, images, and thoughts to concede with my desire to express Divine Love. I find pleasure and harmony in life. Love is my true nature, and my true nature is expressed in this event. I am made from Love, and I call upon love from my feelings, images, and thoughts. I love myself. I respect myself. I praise myself. I approve of myself. I stand firm as I declare that all my feelings, images, and thoughts must be in support of the Image in which I am made. With confidence, great joy, and expectancy, I give thanks for Love.

Physical State: Body/Dis-ease/Appearance   Psoriasis
Emotional State: Soul – faith, endurance, valor
Mental State: Mind – guilt, fear, unloved
Spiritual State: Law – Power (undeveloped)

I now still my mind to know that I am unified with the Image in which I am made. I state emphatically that appearances are merely to guide my life to its Divine Purpose. I accept all appearances as good. I use this appearance to restore my feelings, images, and thoughts to the original purpose to experience Divine Power. My innate wisdom gives me the guidance I need to express faith, endurance, and valor. I move to greater heights. My loyalty, belief, and certainty allow me to live from the Image in which I am made. I do not bend under pressure. I stand up definite, assured, and undaunted to face life. I am courageous and fearless. I refute feelings, images, and thoughts of guilt, fear, and being unloved. I support, confirm, and prove that I am innocent, bold, and loved. The Image in which I am made is Love. This idea fills me with honor. I am responsible for my feelings, images, and thoughts, certain that they are my tools to experience Divine Power. I have the conviction that Divine Love heals all, and I am healed. I respect my feelings, images, and thoughts to guide me to express more love. I am gentle with myself. I am lenient in my assessment of my feelings, images, and thoughts. I am assured, certain, and determined to live from the Image in which I am made. I am honest with myself. I love myself. I praise myself. I am overjoyed at my accomplishments in life. I am rewarded by love. I rely upon, trust, and respect the Image in which I am made. I am free. I accept and embrace feelings of faith, trust, and conviction. I have the physical stamina and spiritual fortitude to face all feelings, images, and thoughts. I develop the quality of mind to move with confidence through all experiences. I gain strength of character. I am fearless in my undertakings. I am confident in my ability to rise above any and all situations. I put my trust in the Image in which I am made. I trust my feelings, images, and thoughts to guide me. In gratitude and with a thankful heart, it is finished.

Physical State: Body/Dis-ease/Appearance   Pyorrhea
Emotional State: Soul – discernment, intelligence
Mental State: Mind – procrastination
Spiritual State: Law – Wisdom (undeveloped)

I live in expectation of an enthusiastic and joy filled life. I remain steadfast in my desire to experience Divine Wisdom. I am guided to pathways of peace and security. I am determined to live from the Image in which I am made. I have the capacity, sagacity, and comprehension of who I am. I recognize my feelings, images, and thoughts to discover the Image in which I am made. Discernment and Intelligence rise out of the Image in which I am made. I perceive the truth of me. I discern my feelings, images, and thoughts to experience Divine Wisdom. I do not accept procrastination in determining my course in this event. I accept expeditious thoughts and action. I take charge of my life and move through this experience in peace. I resolve to live from the Image in which I am made with clarity of purpose. I distinguish my feelings, images, and thoughts to experience Divine Wisdom. I hasten this process. I have the prudence to observe my thoughts to develop the skill of discernment. I view all experiences as favorable, trustworthy, and as evidence of the Image in which I am made. My vision keeps me aware of my power to succeed. My acceptance of my power of good assures my progress. I affirm and resolutely declare that truth, understanding, and order govern my feelings, images, and thoughts. I perceive the truth. I am at ease in allowing my feelings, images, and thoughts to direct my life. They are my indicators of the Image in which I am made. I remove all judgment from my world and live from the Image in which I am made. I am free to experience Divine Wisdom. I abstain from dwelling upon thoughts of distrust, suspicion, and disapproval. I persist and dwell upon thoughts of trust, discernment, and Intelligence. I am aware, alert, and awake. I become patient and submissive to the Image in which I am made. I am at peace. I rest. I am now free to live the totality of life from the Image in which I am made.

Physical State: Body/Dis-ease   Respiratory
Emotional State: Soul – awe, reverence, tranquility
Mental State: Mind – confusion, dread, anxiety
Spiritual State: Law – Love (undeveloped)

I reestablish my divinity and merge with the Image in which I am made. I now embrace all feelings, images, and thoughts to experience Divine Love. I become patient with myself. I am humble in my approach to the Image in which I am made. My perception of good is based upon my desire to unfold my greatest potential. I have all that I require to accomplish my heart's desire. I am created out of love; love is the very life of me. I revere the life of me as I worship the Image in which I am made. I look to myself for completion. I regard each idea in high esteem as my vision of my Divine nature comes to mind. I am in awe, reverence, and tranquility as I embrace Divine Love. I am enthusiastic as I honor the Image in which I am made. I am composed. I refute the appearance of confusion, dread, and anxiety as I equally approve of feelings, images, and thoughts of clarity, boldness, and ease. I face life with confidence, assurance, and valor to express Divine Love. I hold my feelings, images, and thoughts in high regard, as I transpose my thoughts to encourage, comfort, and smooth the way to express Divine Love. I am filled with valor. I am gentle with myself. I feel secure. I reassure myself that I have the capacity to express Divine Love. My feelings, images, and thoughts are pleasing, agreeable, and comforting. I am encouraged to experience Divine love through the Image in which I am made. I am brave, fearless, and undaunted in my resolve to live from the Image in which I am made. I approve of my feelings, images, and thoughts, as they are my guides to expressing love from the Image in which I am made. I find equanimity in all my activities. I am free. I love and forgive myself for not understanding my feelings, images, and thoughts as tools to lead me to the Image in which I am made. I allow the qualities of the Image in which I am made to flow through me to experience Divine Love. In confidence and praise for this realization of the truth about who I am, I am free.

Physical State: Body/Dis-ease/Appearance   Rheumatism
Emotional State: Soul – harmony, ecstasy, rapture
Mental State: Mind – bitterness, animosity, vexation
Spiritual State: Law – Joy (undeveloped)

I know that I am made in the Image and Likeness of Perfection, and I claim my rightful heritage now. I participate in thoughts that are certain and reliable. I embrace and stabilize my feelings, images, and thoughts, which are life giving and life serving, to unify my life. Nothing is too great for me to accomplish. I am enough. I share my talents and abilities with the world. My highest potential unfolds through my feelings, images, and thoughts to express Divine Joy. I give love to myself and recognize that love in all others. I appreciate myself. I praise myself. I welcome the experience of harmony, ecstasy and rapture to uncover the Image in which I am made. I am in agreement with my feelings, images, and thoughts as I experience bliss and euphoria. I am peaceful, happy, and satisfied with this event to express Divine Joy. I refuse to entertain feelings, images, and thoughts of bitterness, animosity, and vexation. I accept thoughts of delight, good will, and contentment. I am sympathetic with my feelings, images, and thoughts. I am kind and patient. I embrace thoughts that are pleasant and pleasurable. I am filled with joy. Divine Joy flows from the Image in which I am made to move through this and all events. I look for and see the truth in all feelings, images, and thoughts to guide me to the Image in which I am made. I seek the good in life to express Divine Joy. I court feelings to bring out the goodness from the Image in which I am made. I am now free to love. I expect love to precede me. My feelings, images, and thoughts are my indicators of my aliveness. I appreciate, honor, and approve of all thoughts that are in harmony with my true nature. I hold my feelings, images, and thoughts in high regard. My thoughts stimulate my feelings, creating greater understanding for a more expansive live. I now take charge of my feelings, images, and thoughts to express Divine Joy to govern my life. In thanksgiving and praise for the Image in which I am made, I am joyful.

Physical State: Body/Dis-ease/Appearance   Sciatica
Emotional State: Soul – unity, discernment, awareness
Mental State: Mind – frustration, scattered thinking
Spiritual State: Law – Wisdom (undeveloped)

I express the Wholeness of life from the Image in which I am made. I live constantly in the midst of good as Divine Wisdom flows through me from the Image in which I am made. I am blessed. I open up to receive graciously and gratefully. My knowing is now established in the Image in which I am made, and I rest. Divine Wisdom brings ideas of freedom and joy from the Image in which I am made. Before I speak, my good is established as I attract what I desire to be expressed from the Image in which I am made. As I unify with the Image in which I am made, discernment and awareness of Divine Power flow through me. I perceive the purpose of this event and realize the need to express Divine Wisdom. I no longer harbor feelings, images, and thoughts of frustration and scattered thinking. I cherish feelings, images, and thoughts of aid support, and regard to live from the Image in which I am made. I am free to change my feelings, images, and thoughts at will. I do so now. I accept and dwell upon thoughts that support the full expression an abundant life. I am composed as I observe the change in my life. My feelings, images, and thoughts cooperate, encourage, and stimulate me to live from the Image in which I am made. I take deliberate action to collect knowledge and focus my attention upon my experience of Divine Wisdom. I perceive with the aid of the Image in which I am made. I center my attention upon that Image and relax. I expect, regard, and incorporate my skills and abilities to experience Divine Wisdom. I meet all my needs to live from the Image in which I am made, and I am peace. I am aware, alert, and awake to the Image in which I am made, and for this I am grateful. I govern my feelings, images, and thoughts to express Divine Wisdom. I receive and identify with all feelings, images, and thoughts of assistance and support to allow me to live from the Image in which I am made. My feelings come to me for furtherance in recognition of the Image in which I am made. In gratitude and thanksgiving, I embrace wisdom.

Physical State: Body/Affairs   Selflessness
Emotional State: Soul — unity, alliance, wholeness
Mental State: Mind — avaricious, venal, covetous
Spiritual State: Law — Peace (undeveloped)

I now empty my mind of turmoil and confusion. I unify my feelings, images, and thoughts and take dominion to allow light to flow through me. I am influenced by the Image of Perfection. I am in agreement with that Image. I am the Essence of that Image; therefore, I am one with all Life. I refuse to dwell upon thoughts of avarice, venality, and covetousness as necessary to express Divine Peace. I accept, dwell and court thoughts of generosity, benevolence, and bounty to support that Image. I am liberal in my assessment of my feelings, images, and thoughts. I am one with my world of effects. I am whole. I am complete. I am sound. I am united with my feelings, images, and thoughts. I embrace feelings that are competent, capable, and appropriate to govern my world. I give love and respect to myself and all others and project the essence of Divine Peace toward everyone I meet. My thoughts are mighty; I think with clarity and precision. I am conscious of my partnership with myself and have an equal share of the unlimited abundance of this world; therefore, I give freely as I receive freely. I am Selfless. That which is mine comes to me easily and freely. I no longer withhold my good. Divine Peace comes to me as I embrace these ideas of life. I trust my inner strength and move with grace and ease. I am altruistic in my assessment of my feelings, images, and thoughts. I am lighthearted and joyous in my giving and receiving. I hold to my awareness of my unity with Life. I trust my feelings, images, and thoughts to bring me to the place where I radiate Divine Peace. I am grateful for this experience to express Divine Peace, and I am abundantly supplied.

Physical State: Body/Dis-ease/Appearance   Shingles
Emotional State: Soul – enthusiasm, fervor, ecstasy
Mental State: Mind – apathy, separation
Spiritual State: Law – Power (undeveloped)

I embrace the Image in which I am made to express Divine Power. I call upon and claim my gift to live from the Image in which I am made. Realizing the purpose of this event, my feelings, images, and thoughts cooperate with my purpose. Appearance and facts can be changed to truth, and I change all appearances and facts now. I am part of the Whole and as such, eternal, never changing. This knowledge stabilizes my thought and gives me more freedom to express Divine Power. I clear my mind to accept the flow of Divine Power. Enthusiasm, fervor, and zeal rise out of the Image in which I am made. Therefore, I am eager, passionate, and filled with rapture to experience Divine Power. I refuse to give in to feelings, images, and thoughts of apathy and separation. I accept and embrace thoughts of interest and unity. I concern myself with my purpose to live from the Image in which I am made. I am filled with zest, vigor and vitality. I want to live. I love life. My feelings, images, and thoughts are warm and responsive to my purpose to live from the Image in which I am made. I am active, participating in this event to live from the Image in which I am made. I am accurate in my assessment of my feelings, images, and thoughts to express Divine Power. I cooperate with myself. I love myself. I praise myself. That Image is immediate and complete. Its Law is now in operation in my life, and I accept the results. I am zealous, dauntless, and filled with courage. I express Divine Power as I integrate my feelings, images, and thoughts to unify with my purpose. I am one with the Image in which I am made. I have never been separated, and I change my feelings, images, and thoughts right now to experience the unity of my being. I nurture my feelings, images, and thoughts to flow with my purpose. I remove all judgment from them and praise who I am. I am the light in my world, and I allow my light to shine. I give thanks for this opportunity to increase my livingness, and for being alive.

Physical State: Body/Dis-ease   Shoulder
Emotional State: Soul – inspiration, hope, courage
Mental State: Mind – burdened, suppressed, restricted
Spiritual State: Law – Power (undeveloped)

I take government over my feelings, images, and thoughts to experience Divine Power. I uphold my promise to myself to live from the Image in which I am made. I have the confidence, encouragement, and freedom to live from the Image in which I am made. I clear my mind to know this right now. My feelings, images, and thoughts are my signal to live from the Image in which I am made. I am capable and emotionally secure in expressing from the Image in which I am made. I willingly allow experiences of power to be incorporated into my every feeling, image, and thought. I welcome the experience of inspiration, hope, and courage to live from the Image in which I am made. I am stimulated as my faith is strengthened, and I draw upon my courage. I deny the experience of burden, suppression, and restriction as necessary to express Divine Power. I declare, assert, and approve of feelings, images, and thoughts of freedom, revealing, and expansion to live from the image in which I am made. Divine Power flows through me. I have respect, reassurance, and confirmation from the Image in which I am made to move through this event with ease. I sustain, support, and promote feelings, images, and thoughts that are bold, secure, and stable. I preserve and maintain my resolve to express Divine Power. This experience is to aid me in fulfilling my heart's desire to express Divine Power from the Image in which I am made. I rise above the sense of separation between my feelings, images, and thoughts. I stand my ground. I take charge. I am free to experience Divine Power as I walk in confidence. I entertain thoughts of bravery, boldness, and dauntlessness to experience Divine Power. I accept feelings, images, and thoughts of allegiance, accountability, and fulfillment as I uncover the Image in which I am made. I have Divine Power to liberate me from judgments I have placed on my feelings, images, and thoughts. I rest in the Image in which I am made.

Physical State: Body/Dis-ease   Sinuses
Emotional State: Soul – enthusiasm, zeal, passion
Mental State: Mind – apathy, torpor, lethargy
Spiritual State: Law – Life (undeveloped)

I am honorable in my intent to uncover the essence of Life through my feelings, images, and thoughts. I am faithful and true to my intent. I face this experience squarely. I see the purpose of my feelings, images, and thoughts. The Source of my life is the Image in which I am made. I move with certainty. I raise the image of myself to one of confidence and significance. I am self-assured. I now see with clarity my uniqueness. I am fortified by the knowledge that I am made in the Image of Perfection. I elevate my mind to accept my feelings, images, and thoughts to experience Divine Power. I am filled with enthusiasm, zeal, and passion. I now turn in devotion to receive the fervor and ecstasy that flows from the Image in which I am made. I refuse to believe the appearance of apathy, torpor, and lethargy. I accept interest, energy, and activity to experience Divine Life. I praise who I am. I am loyal to my purpose. I embrace that which is vital. I stand in awe of Divine Life. I rely upon my feelings, images, and thoughts of trust, credence, and faith. I depend upon my feelings, images, and thoughts to guide me to the full experience of Divine Life. I call upon the beauty of this experience as I seek and find my purpose in it. My duty is to uncover my feelings, images, and thoughts about life and embrace the power to live a life of peace. I am responsible for my feelings, images, and thoughts. I take charge. I give order to my life to express Divine Life and to live from the Image in which I am made. I am faithful and honest in my assessment to bring forth my highest potential through my feelings, images, and thoughts. I serve life with a joyous heart and a willing mind. I am in divine accord with my world. My faith sustains my expectancy. I know that every experience is the letting go of the lesser for the higher—the good for the best.

Physical State: Body/Dis-ease   Skin
Emotional State: Soul – virtue, trust, integrity
Mental State: Mind – guilt, irritation, blame
Spiritual State: Law – Peace (undeveloped)

The image in which I am made allows me to speak these words confidently. My feelings, images, and thoughts are now ordered. I acknowledge the appearance of war in my world, however, appearances are facts and facts can be changed with truth. My purpose is to change facts now with words of truth. I am to experience virtue, trust and integrity through this event. I embrace honesty, confidence and sincerity in this event. I have a Divine Purpose that is now revealed though the Image in which I am made. All feelings, images and thought come to support me in expressing Divine Peace in my world of affairs. Guilt, irritation and blame are not necessary. I embrace innocence, soothing, and praise for my feelings, images, and thoughts. I honor, glorify, and revere the Image in which I am made. I value, extol, and commend the Image in which I am made. I regard, faithfully with ease, the Image in which I am made. I turn in worship to the Image in which I am made. I am worthy. I delight in expressing Divine Peace to soothe my feelings, images, and thought. I have the sufficiency. I accept thoughts of harmony, alliance, and honesty for me to experience the Image in which I am made. I have the confidence, competence, and persistence to express Divine Peace. I unify my feelings, images and thoughts to bring harmony and agreement to live from the Image in which I am made. All feelings, images, and thoughts are in cooperation with the Image in which I am made. All feelings, images, and thoughts benefit me as I see the good in each as part of my purpose to express Divine Peace. I am tranquil, quiet, and reposed in thought. I purify my thoughts to express Divine Peace. My blessings are abundant. The benefits are to experience peace and harmony with my feelings, images, and thoughts. Divine Peace makes its home in my soul. I am at peace. I am still. I am serene and joyous.

Physical State: Body/Dis-ease/Appearance   Snoring
Emotional State: Soul – devotion, reverence, order
Mental State: Mind – aversion, inconsistency, disorder
Spiritual State: Law – Love (undeveloped)

I am in love with Life. I embrace the Image in which I am made to express Divine Love. I court feelings, images, and thoughts about love and become devoted to bringing them in unison with the Image in which I am made. I am privileged to know fulfillment in love. I have the capacity to bring out the essence of passion in my desire to express Divine Love. I especially honor myself in this experience, and I allow Divine Love to flow into every feeling, image, and thought. I turn within in devotion and reverence, with faith and deep respect for the Image in which I am made. I focus on that Image. I am attentive to that Image. I rededicate myself to the Image in which I am made. My allegiance is to the Image in which I am made. I refute feelings, images, and thoughts of aversion, inconsistency, and disorder in my life. I accept and approve feelings of willingness, consistency, and order. I am earnest and honest in my assessments of my feelings, images, and thoughts. I remove all judgment and praise myself for the Image in which I am made. My feelings, images, and thoughts service me, as that is my signal to live from the Image in which I am made. I remain calm, seeking perfect understanding in all events. I remain confident, knowing my gift of love furnishes the right ideas to assuage my feelings, images, and thoughts. I am wise and judicious in determining my purpose to express Divine Love. I am filled with zeal and sincerity, and I adhere to my desire to uncover all feelings, images, and thoughts to reveal Divine Love. I am capable of expressing Divine Love from the Image in which I am made. I experience fervor. I am attracted to feelings, images, and thoughts of love. I direct my attention to developing patterns to express love in all that I do. I am active and alive with an intense desire to develop the Image in which I am made. I use my feelings, images, and thoughts to accomplish my special purpose to radiate Divine Love. I give thanks for this opportunity to uncover the Image in which I am made.

Physical State: Body/Dis-ease/Appearance   Sore Throat
Emotional State: Soul – ecstasy, rapture, exultation
Mental State: Mind – distressed, irritated, irked
Spiritual State: Law – Peace (undeveloped)

I now move with ease, grace, and security from the Image in which I am made to express Divine Peace. I view this event in agreement with the Divine Purpose of my life. I utilize my feelings, images, and thoughts to guide me to the Image in which I am made. I am devoted to the complete enfoldment of the Image in which I am made. I take delight in experiencing events that bring opportunities to express Divine Peace. I am friendly in my approach to my feelings, images, and thoughts to express Divine Peace. I am secure and calm in exercising my Divine Right to express Divine Peace. I am gentle, gracious, and devoted to the Image in which I am made to experience Divine Peace. I embrace feelings, images, and thoughts of ecstasy, rapture, and exultation to experience Divine Peace. I am rewarded with feelings, images, and thoughts of bliss, elation, and joy. I am at peace. I deny distress, irritation, and irked feelings, images, and thoughts. I affirm, court, and honor comfortable, delightful, and cheerful feelings and thoughts to move me through this event. I rejoice in who I am. I take solace in knowing the Image in which I am made. I gain relief. I am serene, delighted, and pleased with my feelings, images, and thoughts to express Divine Peace. My actions are based upon my loyalty to the Image in which I am made. I stand firm in my conviction to fulfill my duty to express Divine Peace. I am one with love, with faith, and with peace. I am aware of my partnership with the Image in which I am made. I am conscious of divine guidance, happiness, and joy. I surround my feelings, images, and thoughts with friendship, love, and beauty. My action is governed by pure Intelligence from the Image in which I am made. I am guided into right action. Enthusiastic joy, vitality, and inspiration are laced into all my activities. I surrender completely in faith to the Image in which I am made. I expect greater good, more happiness, and complete success in every venture. In quiet confidence, faith, and love, I give thanks.

Physical State: Body/Affairs   Splendor
Emotional State: Soul – magnificence, grandeur
Mental State: Mind – repulsive, frightful
Spiritual State: Law – Beauty (undeveloped)

I open my eyes to see the beauty of this world. I gain excellent benefit from this experience. I am made in the Image of Perfection, and I draw upon that Image to change my view of my feelings, images, and thoughts as they are my guides to express Divine Beauty. The attribute of beauty is an asset, and I guard my assets well. It is suitable for me to assess my feelings, images, and thoughts through the eyes of beauty. I see the magnificence of this event as a road map for me to express Divine Beauty. I am important to this world, and I praise myself for my ability to see the splendor, magnificence, and grandeur of this world. I reject thoughts that are repulsive and frightful. I accept and welcome thoughts that are noble, majestic, and transcendent. Appearances are not real. I change my perception of this event and embrace feelings, images, and thoughts that are in harmony with the Image of Perfection. I am at peace. I am filled with enthusiasm as I assess my feelings, images, and thoughts to rise and see the beauty of this event. I am calm. I am cheerful. I embrace noble thoughts. I accept appealing, pleasant, and likeable thoughts, and I follow through with action. I now see through the Image of Perfection and the beauty of the world around me. I change my view. I behold the beauty of my world and see good in every feeling, image, and thought. I am agreeable, friendly, and compassionate in discerning my world of affairs. I embrace expansive and encouraging thoughts to shape my world of beauty. I rise above all limitation to envision my potential to express Divine Beauty.

Physical State: Body/Dis-ease/Appearance   Sprains
Emotional State: Soul – dedication, grace, zeal
Mental State: Mind – resistant, disagreeable, protesting
Spiritual State: Law – Power (undeveloped)

I am made in the Image and likeness of Perfection, and I accept my heritage now. I accept and perceive this Image and welcome it as the Reality of my life. I now place opportunities in the realm of possibility that I have judged beyond my ability to achieve. I now know that the way is provided as the means through the Image in which I am made. I consciously bring myself into harmony with my feelings, images, and thoughts. I change the facts in my life right now by removing all judgments from my feelings, images, and thoughts. I accept my good right now. I rededicate myself to bringing grace and zeal from the Image in which I am made. I commit myself to feelings, images, and thoughts that bring mercy and enthusiasm into my world. I refuse to believe resistance, disagreeableness, and protesting are necessary to express Divine Power. I accept and court feelings, images, and thoughts of surrender, endorsement, and approval of the Image in which I am made. I acquiesce to the Image in which I am made. My feelings, images, and thoughts comply, yield to, and acknowledge my desire to express Divine Power. I have fervor, support, and help to experience Divine Power. I am free to yield, submit, and devote myself to uncovering the Image in which I am made. It is my duty to remove all judgment placed upon my feelings, images, and thoughts. Divine Power flows through me. I expand my efforts for my feelings, images, and thoughts to accomplish my purpose. I indulge in feelings that give strength, vigor, and power. I resolve to express Divine Power from the Image in which I am made. I consent, foster, and promote my desire to express Divine Power. I welcome the opportunity. I agree, accede and allow the Image in which I am made to flow through me. I am profitable. I resign myself to living from the Image in which I am made. I gratefully give thanks and accept the restoration of this event to express Divine Power.

Physical State: Body/Dis-ease/Appearance   Stomach
Emotional State: Soul – order, faith, tranquility
Mental State: Mind – devious, furtive, covert
Spiritual State: Law – Peace (undeveloped)

Divine Peace is in the Image in which I am made and I desire to live from that Image. I am made to express Divine Peace and to participate in the pleasures of life. I tell myself the truth and accept my duty to express from the Image in which I am made. My feelings, images, and thoughts lead me to the Image in which I am made. I remove judgment as I assess my thoughts to express Divine Peace. All thoughts are salutary and genuine. I find comfort and ease as I praise the Image in which I am made. I rejoice in my ability to experience cheerfulness, happiness, and bliss. I demonstrate a love for the Image in which I am made. I am gentle with my feelings, images, and thoughts as I assess the nature of this event. I select thoughts to enhance my self-confidence and self worth. I see through the eyes of love and beauty. My judgments are made with discernment, benevolence, and moral excellence. I now bring order, faith, and tranquility to my feelings, images, and thoughts to express Divine Peace. I structure my life to have confidence and serenity to live from the image in which I am made. I acknowledge feelings, images, and thoughts of deviousness, furtiveness, and covertness as I admit to thoughts that are forthright, open, and clear. I have the assurance, promise, and trust of the Image in which I am made to express Divine Peace. I am honest, sincere, and calm in my approach to my feelings, images, and thoughts. I am composed, comforted, and at ease with the Image in which I am made. I remove all judgment from my feelings, images, and thoughts. The healing action of the Image in which I am made flows through me. I am worthy, considerate, and gentle with myself in my interpretation of my feelings, images, and thoughts. I embrace and find pleasure in living from the Image in which I am made. Divine Peace flows through me. I place trust and gratitude in the Image in which I am made.

Physical State: Body/Dis-ease/Appearance   Stroke
Emotional State: Soul – mastery, trust
Mental State: Mind – resistance, violence, pressure
Spiritual State: Law – Peace (undeveloped)

I have dominion over my feelings, images, and thoughts. I am obedient to the Image in which I am made. I have the ability and acumen to express Divine Peace from the Image in which I am made. I have been given dominion over my feelings, images, and thoughts to express Divine Peace. I have confidence, expectancy, and understanding of the Image in which I am made. My purpose in this event is to express Divine Peace. I now seize this opportunity to comprehend the true purpose of this event. I am obedient to the Image in which I am made. I have all the faith I need in the Image in which I am made. I refuse to believe thoughts of resistance, violence, and pressure as necessary to express Divine Peace. Thoughts of compliance, obedience, and surrender are mine to accomplish living from the Image in which I am made. Gentle, kind, and amicable feelings, images, and thoughts pervade my mind to express Divine Peace. I trust, believe, and am pleased to express Divine Power. I embrace this event to accomplish my innate desire to live from the Image in which I am made. I welcome the activity of Divine Peace. I take delight in and expect my feelings, images, and thoughts to lead me to the Image in which I am made. I am fulfilled. I am prospered. I flourish. I move with a certainty to restore my feelings, images, and thoughts to execute Divine Peace. I am brave. I comprehend my purpose in this experience to express Divine Peace. I thrive upon the Image in which I am made to express the qualities of Divine Peace. I move forward in faith, accepting the Image in which I am made as who I am. Divine Joy fills my being. I relax and rest in sweet repose. I open up to receive the essence of the Image in which I am made to experience Divine Peace. I am at peace. I embrace peace to restore my feelings, images, and thoughts to the original purpose to express Divine Peace. I now give thanks for the realization of the purpose for this event.

Physical State: Body/Dis-ease/Appearance   Suicidal
Emotional State: Soul – gratitude, hope, trust
Mental State: Mind – inactive, inadequate, weary
Spiritual State: Law – Life (undeveloped)

I want to live from the Image in which I am made. This event is my heart's desire to live from the Image in which I am made. I want to succeed. I draw upon the Image in which I am made to lead guide and direct my paths to a more gracious living. I acknowledge my purpose. I am important to myself and to the world. I have faith that I can succeed in expressing Divine Life. I move beyond my feelings, images, and thoughts to recognize my value to this world. I am stimulated by my acknowledgement of the Image in which I am made. My confidence is restored in me. I believe in myself. I trust myself. I participate in life. I am substantial. I have the expectancy of change. I am filled with veracity, verve and vigor to express Divine Life. Hence my feelings, images, and thoughts of inactivity, inadequacy and weariness are no longer active in my life. Feelings, images and thought of activity, competence and revival now pervade my mind. I embrace life. I am now aware of the Image in which I am made and vow to myself to live from that Image. I am beneficial. I embrace feelings, images, and thoughts of activity, excitement and amusement to experience Divine Life. I claim my privilege to draw upon my inherent powers of boldness, daring and duration to live from the Image in which I am made. I am filled with zest and zeal. I seek activities that are interesting, lively, and stimulating. I am relieved. I draw upon the Intelligence within the Image in which I am made for direction. I receive new ideas. I take action upon those ideas. I am now in harmony with the Image in which I am made. I draw upon the vitality of my being. I now give thanks for the realization of my purpose, as I embrace life.

Physical State: Body/Dis-ease/Appearance   Swelling
Emotional State: Soul – passion devotion, rapture
Mental State: Mind – dread, disgust, apathy
Spiritual State: Law – Love (undeveloped)

I now recommit myself to myself to live from the Image in which I am made. I become increasingly aware of my purpose to express Divine Love through this event. I place my faith in my feelings, images, and thoughts to lead, guide and direct me to activity to express Divine Love. Love heals all wounds. As I focus my attention upon loving actions, passion, devotion and rapture fills my world to express Divine Love. These qualities are in the Image in which I am made and I draw upon that part of me right now. I am filled with the essence of enthusiasm, commitment and rapture fills my being. I reject dread, disgust and apathy as real or valid in this life. I accept only feelings, images, and thoughts of courage, earnestness, and interest to express Divine Love. I now move into the Image in which I am made to express Divine Love. I am pleased, earnest, and fervent to revel in Divine Love. I seek activities to impress upon my feelings images to experience Divine Love. I remain eager and steadfast to my purpose. I take great pleasure in expressing Divine Love. I have reverence for the Image in which I am made. I adhere to my duty to express Divine Love. I am filled with zest and zeal, which come to support me in expressing Divine Love. My feelings, images, and thoughts are now in alignment with the Image in which I am made. I am energized and bold in my effort to express Divine Love. I am attracted to images, feelings, and thoughts of love and direct my attention to developing a pattern to express love in all that I do, say, or think. My feelings, images, and thoughts are my tools to accomplish my special purpose to radiate Divine Love. I am grateful for the knowledge of the truth about me.

Physical State: Body/Affairs   Sympathy
Emotional State: Soul – harmony, amity, empathy
Mental State: Mind – disapproval, disfavor
Spiritual State: Law – Joy (undeveloped)

Right now, I see through the eyes of the Image of Perfection and realize my unity with all Life. I see the truth and I am free. The Life force that is within me is the same Life Force in everyone and everything. I claim that Life right now and unify my feeling, images and thought. I see the simple acts that fill my days and know that all actions are for my highest good. I am filled with joy. I am in agreement with Life. Cooperation, understanding and compassion are the foundation of that Image of Perfection. I refuse to believe thoughts of disapproval and disfavor is necessary for me to express Divine Joy. I affirm and embrace thoughts of approval, accord and kindness in support of my desire to express Divine Joy. I have regard for my life. I participate in my life. I am in agreement with Life and take pleasure in discerning my feelings, images and thought to express Divine Joy. I recognize opportunities to express Divine Joy in my daily living. My thoughts give me awareness of Joy for the renewing of my mind. I think with clarity. I am advised, encouraged and supported by my thoughts and I honor each one. I have assurance through my trust in my feelings, images, and thoughts to express Divine Joy as I participate in activities that bring cheerful encounters. I accept feelings of expectation and enthusiasm. I open up to receive Divine Joy in my world. I am active and alive with an intense desire to develop my true nature as an Image of Perfection. I am sincere in my desire and develop a passion to express Divine Joy in everything I do. I love myself. I bless myself and all others as I give thanks to express Divine Joy.

Physical State: Body/Dis-ease   Throat
Emotional State: Soul – discernment, order, tranquility
Mental State: Mind – anger, hurt, confusion
Spiritual State: Law – Wisdom (undeveloped)

I seek to know the Image in which I am made through this event and heal my feelings, images, and thoughts to express Divine Wisdom. I have the perception, depth of understanding and keen insight to accomplish my desire. I trust my feelings, images, and thoughts to guide me. I listen and I obey. I am motivated and stimulated by the Image in which I am made. I remove all barriers and allow Divine Wisdom to fill my thoughts with substance and faith. I strive for understanding and endeavor to use it in my relationship with my feelings, images, and thoughts. All experiences are good. All that I desire and embody is in the Image in which I am made. I incorporate in my experience what I will take and use. I meet all experiences with poise and assurance. I focus my attention upon the Image in which I am made to heal this appearance. I surrender all feelings, images, and thoughts to live from the Image in which I am made. I deny all appearance of having throat trouble. My purpose in this event is to allow for the essence of discernment, order, and tranquility to express as Divine Wisdom. I perceive enlightenment and serenity in this event. I refuse to accept anger, hurt, and confusion as necessary to express Divine Wisdom. I accept, love, relief, and composure to express Divine wisdom. I am free in my expression as I declare my purpose to live from the Image in which I am made. I rethink my faith in myself. I love myself. I am serene. My desire to live from the Image in which I am made is profound. I seek enlightenment and direct communication from the Image in which I am made. I am wise, astute, and I have the acumen to express Divine Love. In gratitude and thanksgiving, I accept Divine Wisdom.

Physical State: Body/Dis-ease   Thyroid
Emotional State: Soul - tranquility, discernment, praise
Mental State: Mind – anger, hurt, confusion
Spiritual State: Law – Love (undeveloped)

I take great pleasure in uncovering my innate qualities to express Divine Love. I declare for myself the right to express Divine Love. I reorder my feelings, images, and thoughts to embrace the Image in which I am made. I am serene. I am tranquil and still. I am vital, safe, and wise in my decision to live from the Image in which I am made. I am pleasantly delighted and soothed. I embrace peace. I ascertain Divine Love through praise and worship for the Image in which I am made. I deny anger, hurt, and confusion to express Divine Love. I affirm and emphatically state love, compliments, and praise for the Image in which I am made. I praise, laude, and console my feelings, images, and thoughts for this to guide me to the Image in which I am made. I remove judgment from my feelings, images, and thoughts to embrace the Image in which I am made. I recognize my feelings, images, and thoughts as my guidepost to express Divine Love. I participate in acts of love, compliments, and refinement to celebrate the Image in which I am made. I radiate my love for my feelings, images, and thoughts in all that I do. I am enough. I seize every opportunity to learn though experience the meaning of love. I am the governor of my feelings, images, and thoughts. I hold firm to thoughts of honesty and truth to live from the Image in which I am made. I see with clarity. I accept the Image in which I am made. I move boldly, confidently, and with certainty through this experience to align with the Image in which I am made. Divine Love fills my thoughts with the love for life. I have a sense of security as I trust the Image in which I am made.

Physical State: Body/Dis-ease   Toe
Emotional State: Soul – symmetry, equanimity, poise
Mental State: Mind – anxious, apprehensive, fearful
Spiritual State: Law – Peace (undeveloped)

I am free. This is the truth, and I willingly face the Image in which I am made and govern my life in harmony with It. I stand firm in my conviction to uncover the Image in which I am made. I am stabilized in the power of Divine Peace. Right now, in the intimate quiet of this moment, I experience peace. The Image in which I am made is the source of all inspiration, illumination, and revelation. Everything I need to know is revealed to me. I dwell, live, and rest within the Image in which I am made. I regain my balance, composure, and assurance. I find stability, harmony, and confidence in the Image I am made. Therefore, I refuse to accept anxiousness, apprehensiveness, or fear. I make firm in my mind thoughts that relieve, assure, and calm my feelings, images, and thoughts. I am confident in my ability to express Divine Peace. I am courageous, bold, and brave. I am in harmony to unfold the Image in which I am made. I submit totally to the express divine Peace. I remain steadfast, unchangeable in my desire to live from the Image in which I am made. I praise who I am. I am in harmony with my feelings, images, and thoughts to express Divine Peace. I am flexible, self confident and considerate. I am reliable. My perception is clear. My purpose is certain. I welcome opportunities to live from the Image in which I am made. I have the capacity, skill, and aptness to experience Divine Peace. I remove all judgment from my feelings, images, and thoughts to experience Divine Peace. I am thankful and inspired by the revelations of the Image in which I am made.

Physical state: Body/Dis-ease   Tongue
Emotional State: Soul – truth, splendor, Reality
Mental State: Mind – conflict, opposition, hypocrisy
Spiritual State: Law – Beauty (undeveloped)

I am the light of my world. I draw to myself that which I need to live from the Image in which I am made. I tell myself the truth about this event. I live from integrity and honesty with myself. I am accountable only to the Image in which I am made. I am loyal and trustworthy. I call upon my innate qualities to express Divine Beauty. Truth transcends all events as I perceive Reality. I am accurate in my assessment of my feelings, images, and thoughts to express Divine Beauty. I refute thoughts of conflict, opposition, and hypocrisy. I accept and embrace thoughts that agree, support, and are genuine in my expression of Divine Beauty. I see the good in this event. I am honorable, sincere, and trustworthy. I bring joy to my life. My communication is authentic. I depend upon the Image in which I am made to lead, guide, and direct my every action. I see the splendor in all things to express Divine Beauty. My feelings, images, and thoughts are now in alignment with my purpose to live from the Image in which I am made. I decide to see things differently. I honor my feelings, images, and thoughts as my guide to express Divine Beauty. I am accurate in my assessment. I love myself and free myself to embrace Divine Beauty. I am open and receptive to see the beauty in all things. My life reflects the truth of all creation. I see the symmetry in the plant, the rainbow, and the clouds and even in the night sky. I claim dominion over my world. I am unified with ideas of beauty. My feelings, images, and thoughts are in perfect union with the Image in which I am made. I am grateful for this opportunity to express Divine Beauty.

Physical State: Body/Affairs   Transport
Emotional State: Soul —rapture, ecstasy, bliss
Mental State: Mind — sadness, dejection, discouragement
Spiritual State: Law — Divine Joy (undeveloped)

Divine Joy is a gift of Life and I am in perfect and Divine accord with my Life. I am conscious that there is complete unity in my life. This moment, I seek to experience Divine Joy and express this Essence through my feelings, images, and thoughts. I transcend this state of mind to express Divine Joy. Rapture, ecstasy, and bliss are natural states for me to experience Divine Joy. Therefore, I refuse to entertain thoughts of sadness, dejection, and discouragement as I accept and embrace thoughts of happiness, elation, and encouragement. My natural state of being is the Image of Perfection. I am transported to that State to restore my mind to peace and Divine Joy. I take delight in assessing my feelings, images, and thoughts to uncover my true nature to express Divine Joy. I am cheerful, enthusiastic and filled with glee as I move through this experience. I become conscious of who I am and express this knowing in my world of affairs. I give freely to life. I accept joy and happiness at all times and participates in activities that which bring me joy. Life is to be enjoyed and I participate fully in the process of bringing joy into my activities. I set my intention each day to express joy. I look for and find activities to have fun. I no longer expect anyone or anything to bring me Joy. I am Joy. Joy flows through my feelings, images, and thoughts as I change my perspective on the situations in my life. I accept joy. Divine Joy floods my being, and I am transported in my feelings, images, and thoughts to heights of glee. I am happy. My thoughts bring smiles to my face, and others are blessed by my smiles as I radiate Divine Joy. I am grateful for this experience.

Physical State: Body/Dis-ease/Appearance   Tumors
Emotional State: Soul – unity, harmony, reconciliation
Mental State: Mind – hurt, resentment, jealousy
Spiritual State: Law – Peace (undeveloped)

I tell myself the truth. I have all that I need to express Divine Peace and I change my feelings, images, and thoughts right now to reflect peace. I trust the Image in which I am made. I forgive myself. I love and release myself. I embrace my unity, oneness and wholeness to live from the Image in which I am made. I am loyal and honest in assessing my feelings, images, and thoughts to express Divine Peace. I renounce hurts, resentment, and jealousy as necessary to express Divine Peace. I claim and embrace thoughts of ease, rejoicing and trusting as the foundation for my success in expressing Divine Peace. I forgive as I am forgiven. I am in accord with the Image in which I am made. I am accountable to that Image to express Divine Peace. I find contentment in the Image in which I am made. Divine Peace floods my being. I move through this and all events in peace, drawing from the wellspring of the Image in which I am made. I am honorable in viewing my feelings, images, and thoughts as tools for help in expressing Divine Peace. It is natural for me to express Divine Peace. I rest in peace. I have faith in my ability to express Divine Peace. I garner my capabilities of trust. My feelings, images, and thoughts are my guide to live from the Image in which I am made. I honor myself. I am pleased with all feelings, images, and thoughts. I remove all judgment from my feelings and allow Divine Peace to flood my being. I am at ease. I am tranquil. I bring out the essence of joy in every feeling, image, and thought. I welcome all experiences to heal my feelings, images, and thoughts. I am grateful for the realization of the purpose of this event as I praise the Image in which I am made.

Physical State: Body/Dis-ease/Appearance   Ulcer
Emotional State: Soul – rapture, tranquility
Mental State: Mind – pain, worry, agony
Spiritual State: Law – Peace (undeveloped)

It is a relief to know the purpose of this event is to express Divine Peace. I change my feelings, images, and thoughts to agree with my purpose to express Divine Peace. I rejoice in experiencing rapture and tranquility from the Image in which I am made. The essence of joy, ecstasy, and serenity is the reward of expressing Divine Peace. Feelings, images and thought that bring pain, worry, and agony have no place in my life. I welcome thoughts of comfort, self-possession, and enjoyment to fill my mind. I find relief in knowing that I am made in the Image and Likeness of Perfection. I have everything that I need from the Image in which I am made. I claim my inheritance now. I move forward embracing feelings, images, and thoughts which being comfort, relief, and contentment. I am aided in my desire to express Divine Peace. It is desirable and refreshing to know this experience allows me to express Divine Peace in all my affairs. I seize this opportunity cheerfully now that I understand my purpose. I am bold, daring and dauntless as I move thought this event. I am in harmony with my feelings, images, and thoughts, finding assurance and confidence in expressing Divine Peace. I am capable of living from the Image in which I am made. Divine Love supports me. I value my freedom to express Divine Peace. I release this event and live from the Image in which I am made. I rest in sweet repose. Ideas, inspiration and guidance flow from the Image in which I am made. I believe in the power of the Image in which I am made. My way is peaceful. In faith, I am secure. I remain steadfast in my conviction to live from the Image in which I am made.

Physical State: Body/Affairs   Vanity
Emotional State: Soul – self-esteem, worth, meekness
Mental State: Mind – folly, futility, unreality
Spiritual State: Law – Divine Wisdom (undeveloped)

I surrender to the Image of Perfection in which I am made. I court gentleness in speech, consideration of my feelings, and patience in my thought to unfold this Image. I bring forth the dignity of who I am. I am humble in my assessment of my images, feelings and thoughts. I value myself and see the worth in my feelings, images, and thoughts as guidelines for me to express Divine Wisdom. I am humble in my assessment. I refute all thoughts of folly, futility and unreality as necessary for me to experience Divine Wisdom. I affirm, embrace, and marshal thoughts of prudence and sound judgment that are profitable to express Divine Wisdom. My feelings, images, and thoughts are significant to my expression of Divine Wisdom. I tell myself the truth and move through all illusion of impractical actions. I understand facts are necessary to understand my true nature. I embrace feelings of worthiness, submissive only to feelings of joy. I praise my feelings, images, and thoughts. I know who I am. I no longer need to pretend. I am relaxed as I feel the flow of energy to express Divine Wisdom. I am important to this world and I approach life in a simple manner, praising my Image of Perfection. I am humbled. I open up to receive new feelings, images, and thoughts to reclaim my self-worth. I hold myself in high esteem. My feelings bring out the gentleness within me. I am eager to experience reality. I now clear my mind. I am certain of my feelings, images, and thoughts as truth is revealed through me. I praise and support who I am. I approve of myself just as I am. I am effective. My understanding is sound. My thoughts are elevated. My perception is keen. I am grateful.

Physical state: Body/Dis-ease/Appearance   Varicose Veins
Emotional State: Soul – dominion, service, flexibility
Mental State: Mind – resistance, tension, force
Spiritual State: Law – Power (undeveloped)

I allow myself to see the good in this event. I move into the Image in which I am made and claim my heritage. Right now, I restore my feelings, images, and thoughts to adapt to the new knowledge of who I am. I have been given dominion, authority and supremacy over my feelings, images, and thoughts. I order my thinking to move from idea to idea to serve. I am flexible in my movement to express Divine Power. I am effective in my desire to live from the Image in which I am made. I refute feelings, images, and thoughts of resistance, tension and force as necessary to express Divine Power. I embrace thoughts that are flexible, praise-worthy and enthusiastic. Divine Power is my heritage and I express that quality in this event. I am relaxed, calm and at peace. I yield to the Image in which I am made. I have acceptance of my purpose to express Divine Power. I rest in sweet repose. I promote, foster and aid my feelings, images, and thoughts in my effort to live from the Image in which I am made. I am gentle with myself. I love myself. I praise myself. I am adaptable and willing to change my feelings, images, and thoughts to enjoy the benefit of living from the Image in which I am made. I surrender and accept the help needed to express Divine Power. I praise the Image in which I am made. I am alive, aware and awake. I am active with the intense desire to develop my true nature to live from the Image in which I am made. I am at peace. I am courageous, brave, and undaunted. I am grateful for the knowledge of who I am.

Physical State: Body/Dis-ease/Appearance   Vomiting
Emotional State: Soul – tranquility, serenity, freedom
Mental State: Mind – frustration, fear, anxiety
Spiritual State: Law – Wisdom (undeveloped)

I am now open to receive the foresight, good judgment and understanding to live from the Image in which I am made. I am peaceful, calm and self-reliant in assessing my feelings, images, and thoughts to live from the Image in which I am made. I am free. I refuse to believe frustration, fear and anxiety are necessary to express Divine Wisdom. I affirm, court, and dwell upon thoughts that promote, foster, and bring relief. I have confidence in the Image in which I am made to express Divine Wisdom. I liberate, release and emancipate my feelings, images, and thoughts to express Divine Wisdom. I have the assurance, certainty and the perception to restore my body to express Divine Power. I am encouraged. I love myself. I seize upon this event as an opportunity to express Divine Wisdom. I comprehend the truth of who I am and rightly discern the purpose of this event. I am at peace. I console my feelings, images, and thoughts to express Divine Wisdom. My reasoning is clear. My thinking is sound. My understanding is astute. I now adjust my life to express Divine Wisdom. I court gentleness in speech, consideration in feelings and patience in thought to live from the Image in which I am made. I approach life in a simple manner, praising the Image in which I am made. I approve of myself just the way I am. I accept my duty to express from the Image in which I am made. I am modest in assessing my feelings, images, and thoughts to express Divine Wisdom. I am rewarded with the freedom to receive pure Ideas to express Divine Wisdom. I praise who I am. I rejoice in knowing the Image in which I am made. For this, I am thankful.

Physical State: Body/Affairs   Wisdom
Emotional State: Soul – comprehension, sagacity
Mental State: Mind – folly, absurdity
Spiritual State: Law – Divine Wisdom (undeveloped)

This moment, I know that Truth sets me free from doubt, fear and uncertainty. I claim my gift of Wisdom as I seek to understand my Image of Perfection. I open my mind with enthusiasm. I accept Divine Wisdom as it flows through me. I draw upon my foresight and knowledge from my feelings, images, and thoughts to comprehend this experience. I am keenly aware of my innate purpose and I draw upon my wellspring of wisdom to uncover that purpose. I perceive that which is for my highest fulfillment in all situations. I refute thoughts of folly and absurdity as necessary to receive Divine Wisdom. I accept only thoughts of truth, credibility and sagacity to express Divine Wisdom. I am sensible and sound. There is within me a discerning factor that I can draw upon to make wise decisions in my assessment of my feelings, images, and thoughts. I am practical and prudent. I am guided and motivated by that Image of Perfection to conceive of the purpose of each experience. I am vigilant in my desire to uncover my true feelings, images, and thoughts to express Divine Wisdom. I live in a world of unity. I place my trust in Life and I am guided in my understanding. Everything I need to know is made known to me. I see Divine guidance in the world about me. The right answer is within me. I have a deep sense of inner calm – a complete faith in Divine Wisdom as its essence flows through me. I use the knowledge and skills that I have to do what is before me. I feel confident in the action that I take to do that which is for my highest good. I am inspired by my feelings, images, and thoughts as I grasp greater insights. I accept this as truth for me right now as I live from the Image in which I am made.

Physical State: Body/Dis-ease   Wrist
Emotional State: Soul – unity, abundance, gratitude
Mental State: Mind – withdrawn, lacking
Spiritual State: Law – Power (undeveloped)

I let go of myself and surrender to the Image in which I am made. I approve of myself. I love myself. I have balance and a sufficiency of all needs as I draw upon the wellspring of the Image in which I am made. I am poised and rejoice in the ample supply of the Image in which I am made. I have the richness, wealth and opulence of the Image in which I am made. Therefore, feelings, images, and thoughts of being withdrawn and lack have no place in my life. I court, embrace and rely upon thoughts that are assertive and involved in expressing the Image in which I am made. I have the obligation to express Divine Power in my life. I am sustained in my effort to express Divine Power in this event. I feel secure. I am pleased. I accommodate and cooperate with the Image in which I am made by gratefully taking leadership over my feelings, images, and thoughts. I move with authority to express Divine Power. I have the capability to command myself to receive and give from the Image in which I am made. I expand my capacity to experience Divine Power. I am soothe and nurtured by the Image in which I am made. I take great delight in living from the Image in which I am made. My feelings, images, and thoughts guide me. I open up to experience the richness, wealth and opulence of the Image in which I am made. In this moment, my good comes to me, enough and to spare. I give generously as I receive graciously. I recognize my feelings, images, and thoughts as my divine heritage. They are my safeguards, my stepping-stones to live from the Image in which I am made. I am grateful for the knowledge of the Image in which I am made.

Physical State: Body/Affairs   Worry
Emotional State: Soul – solace, calm, assurance
Mental State: Mind – vexation, torment, disgust
Spiritual State: Law – Divine Peace (undeveloped)

I trust life. In faith I am secure. I accept all that I need for inspiration and guidance. I put my trust in the Image of Perfection. I am calm and peaceful. I am comforted by my feelings, images, and thoughts of Divine Peace. I am relieved when I focus on Divine Peace, and I receive assurance from my feelings, images, and thoughts. I refuse to believe thoughts of vexation, torment and disgust as necessary for me to experience Divine Peace. I affirm ease, comfort and joy as my natural inheritance to experience Divine Peace. I am pleased with my feelings, images, and thoughts, as they are my guides to experience Divine Peace. I change my perception of this experience to one of joy and allow Divine Peace to flow through me. I bring out the essence of peace in every thought. I value my freedom to express Divine Peace. Whatever I need has already been provided, and I clear my mind to receive my heart's desire. I welcome thoughts to change false feelings, images, and thoughts about this experience. Thoughts of the Image of Perfection in which I am made refresh me. I stand ready to experience Life. I still my mind and move freely to a place where my thoughts are tranquil, quiet, and still. I am soothed and nurtured by thoughts of Divine Peace. I move through all feelings, images, and thoughts contrary to the Image of Perfection in which I am made. I accept my good. I rest in sweet repose. I accept feelings that bring peace, quietness, and repose. I am pleased with all feelings. I call them good and very good. All appearances not in harmony with my feelings fall away. I am at ease in my world.

Physical state: Body/Dis-ease/Appearance   Yeast Infection
Emotional State: Soul – devotion, rapture
Mental State: Mind – irritation, anger, annoyance
Spiritual State: Law – Power (undeveloped)

The life that is within me is the Image in which I am made and I have reverence for it. It is to that Image I turn my attention and focus. My allegiance is in expressing Divine Power. I am devoted to that Image to experience rapture. I am faithful in my resolve to express Divine Power. Therefore, I refute irritation, anger, and annoyance as true. I embrace, prove, and answer to feelings, images, and thoughts of good nature, love, and pleasure. I have the ability, support, and faith to live from the Image in which I am made. I acknowledge, obey, and respect my feelings, images, and thoughts to express Divine Power. I honor who I am. I appreciate who I am. I regard my feelings, images, and thoughts and accept this event as no longer necessary to express Divine Power. I change my feelings, images, and thoughts to align with the purpose to express Divine Power. I forgive myself. I praise, admire and appreciate the realization for the purpose of this event. I move forward with zeal, ardor and consideration for the Image in which I am made. I am calm. I am at peace. I have an earnest concern for the Image in which I am made. Divine Power leads me and I move in confidence, peace and joy. I keep my thoughts centered upon my purpose to express Divine Power. My response to life is affirmative. I am sustained by Divine power from the Image in which I am made. I am maintained by the Image in which I am made. I move forward with enthusiasm, knowing the purpose for this event. I recommit myself to live from the Image in which I am made. I obey my feelings, images, and thoughts to guide me to the Image in which I am made.

Printed in the United States
By Bookmasters